What people are saying about

Strip: The Making of a Feminist

Catlyn Ladd gives us a compelling and dramatic view into the world of desire. Her journey, mind and body and heart, takes the reader into her experience as a voyeur without judgment and with critical insight. The book is raw, dangerous, sensitive, and real, like the life Ladd portrays. It reads like social science with a storyteller's heart.

Michelle Auerbach, author of *The Third Kind of Horse* and *Alice Modern*

Strip: The Making of a Feminist challenges the patriarchal stereotypes of sexual women as undereducated, manipulative, and exploited. Taking an intersectional approach that considers privileges and oppressions, Ladd offers both her personal history and academic perspective on sex work. This book is not only relevant to the changing landscape of 21st century feminisms, it is useful to all readers who wish to deconstruct their ~~ sexuality.

Neil Cannon, Ph.D., LMFT

Strip: The Making of a Feminist provides ⸌ ⸍ ⸌aɯyıı Ladd's experience stripping over the course of five years. While like other autoethnographic accounts of the strip club industry, Ladd's contribution to the genre involves her incorporation of feminist critique within a sex positive framework. Ladd skillfully explores the nuances of female sexual empowerment while evaluating her own experience as "empowered" within a racist, capitalist, hetero-patriarchal work environment and culture. She reveals that although stripping can empower some women, this empowerment exists within the context of broader social systems that grant certain women the privilege of empowerment. In other words, some women choose to strip out of desire, while others choose to strip out of need, or perhaps do not have a choice. These realizations help Ladd synthesize her experience into a tale of growth, whereby the reader begins with a basic introduction to the industry in Section I and is led through Ladd's growing feminist consciousness in the following sections. It is within these sections we see Ladd explore the contradictions of female sexual empowerment, but it is this exploration that reminds the reader of sex positivity's significance for women in the United States.

Katherine Martinez, Ph.D., author of "BDSM Role Fluidity: A Mixed Methods Approach to Investigating Switches within Dominant/Submissive Binaries," *Journal of Homosexuality* (forthcoming) and "Somebody's Fetish: Self-Objectification and Body Satisfaction among Consensual Sadomasochists," *Journal of Sex Research* (2015).

Strip:
The Making of
a Feminist

Strip:
The Making of
a Feminist

Catlyn Ladd

**CHANGE
MAKERS
BOOKS**

Winchester, UK
Washington, USA

First published by Changemakers Books, 2018
Changemakers Books is an imprint of John Hunt Publishing Ltd., No. 3 East St., Alresford,
Hampshire SO24 9EE, UK
office1@jhpbooks.net
www.johnhuntpublishing.com
www.changemakers-books.com

For distributor details and how to order please visit the 'Ordering' section on our website.

Text copyright: Catlyn Ladd 2017

ISBN: 978 1 78535 737 4
978 1 78535 738 1 (ebook)
Library of Congress Control Number: 2017941346

A CIP catalogue record for this book is available from the British Library.

Design: Stuart Davies

Printed and bound by CPI Group (UK) Ltd, Croydon, CR0 4YY, UK

We operate a distinctive and ethical publishing philosophy in
all areas of our business, from our global network of authors to
production and worldwide distribution.

Contents

For all the powerful, amazing people in the world who choose to do unconventional things.

Acknowledgments

Firstly, I need to acknowledge all of the women and men I worked with in clubs over the course of five years. This is your story almost as much as it is mine. Though this book is written so as to protect the identities of my co-workers and the customers, my experiences with each of you contributed to who I am in my professional, adult life.

Secondly, acknowledgment and thanks go to Tim Ward, my mentor and friend, and author/publisher at Changemakers Books. Tim and I cooked up the idea for this book years ago after I divulged my previous career in sex work. After hearing some of my stories, Tim urged me to begin writing them down.

Thirdly, I am so deeply grateful for my parents and partner. My parents always support me, even when I make choices that make them nervous. My mother spent long hours editing this book for submission and my father and I strategized marketing, design, and philosophy for almost as long. Greg is my magical, wonderful, smart, talented, beautiful partner in life—he always sees the very best in me and holds me to the very highest standard.

I'd be remiss not to give a special shoutout to Robert Linder for his photography skills. Thank you for making me look good!

Finally, a lot of people at Changemakers Books provided invaluable editing, feedback, marketing, insight, and advice. I received rigorous support throughout the publication process. Made the first book seem easy! I am lucky and appreciative.

Section I

Into the Abyss

And if thou gaze long into an abyss, the abyss will also gaze into thee.

—Frederick Nietzsche

Chapter One

The Beginning

The entirety of my wardrobe hangs on a clothes rack occupying one wall of our bedroom. I go through the items rapidly, pulling candidates off the rack and laying them out on the bed, which is a double futon on milk crates. The crates serve the dual function of keeping the bed off the floor and organizing jeans, sweaters, and books. It's college chic.

My boyfriend looks on, sitting on the bed sorting hosiery. He's looking for my garter belt, which has to be mixed in somewhere with the fishnets and thigh-high witch stockings.

"What about this?" I hold up a minidress that zips down the front. One side is black and the other side is white.

"With these." He holds up a pair of black and white striped stockings.

"Those don't match," I say.

"They don't?" He looks at them quizzically.

"No. The stripes are different widths."

"I kind of like that."

"I don't think strippers are supposed to be edgy."

"Well, I'd tip you." He goes back to the pile.

Audrey is picking me up in an hour. My makeup kit is already packed; now I just have to figure out what clothes to take. I have lots of hot pants, miniskirts, and catsuits, but it all looks like club wear to me, something to wear to a rave.

"Ah, ha!" Triumphantly he holds up a garter belt and another striped stocking.

"Add those to that pile." I point to a small collection of clothing that I think will be suitable. I only have one pair of shoes, white sandals with clunky heels that I bought on sale at Wal-Mart for $10. Everything I take tonight has to match and most of my clothes are black.

I put everything in a duffel bag and add my makeup and a curling iron. I throw in a single black velvet thong that I had been able to afford ($5 at Wal-Mart) along with the shoes. I am not nervous, only worried about making money. The idea of being naked in front of strangers doesn't concern me, but I do feel a twinge about my appearance. Loads of people, both men and women, have told me how beautiful I am and intellectually I know that I fit the current social standards for beauty: tall, thin, blond. But my skin isn't perfect, my teeth are crooked, and I worry that my thighs are too thick. Am I good enough to actually earn money at this? I need money badly.

During the 45-minute drive to the club, Audrey coaches me. "Don't call me by my real name," she tells me. "Remember to call me Sierra. Don't steal a customer from another girl. Don't sit at the dressing table until I show you where you can. Never take your top off until the second song. If you're on stage two, don't take your top off until after the girl on stage one takes hers off. You tip out 10% to the bar, 10% to the DJ, and the bouncers get four or five bucks apiece. Don't touch the customers and remember that they can't touch you. Take the money in your G-string; don't let them do it for you."

My head buzzes with all the rules. That's a lot of "don'ts."

"Did you bring a lock?"

"A lock? Um...no."

She shakes her head disparagingly. "Well, there's an empty locker. Just hope your stuff doesn't get stolen. Did you bring a purse?"

"No." I'm still stuck on *stolen*.

"I think I have one I can loan you. Never leave your money in your locker unless it's locked."

"Where do I put it?"

"When you're on stage you can set it next to the stairs. Just keep an eye on it. Some bitches will steal all your shit."

This information conforms to the stereotypes I've picked up from society about women who strip their clothes off for money. In films and television shows, strippers are drug addled, uneducated, trafficked, manipulative, and scorned. Audrey is a year ahead of me in college and is none of those things. But she speaks of her co-workers in ways that seem to confirm the stereotypes.

I don't know what I expect of the club, but I'm surprised when we pull into the parking lot of a strip mall. The club is nestled between a dry-cleaning place and a burger joint. The air smells like grease.

"This the new girl?"

The bouncer looks friendly enough and he smiles at me warmly. "I'm Ken," he says, holding out a hand. "Welcome."

I don't hesitate. "Desire." I had chosen the name from *The Sandman* comics after the androgynous hermaphrodite, sibling to the Dream King.

Ken doesn't even blink. "Welcome. If you need anything please ask."

He seems nice enough. "Thank you," I reply and Sierra pulls me into the club.

Again, not what I expected. The floor is polished concrete. A hardwood bar faces the door. It's shaped like a horseshoe and the portly, balding bartender gives me an unsmiling once-over. Three of the barstools are occupied and the men look at us with more friendly expressions.

"Hey, Sierra," one says. "Who's your friend?"

"Fresh meat," she says with a laugh.

This is not the last time I will be referred to as meat in this industry.

She leads me between a row of high-top tables and then through a maze of small, round tables. They are fake wood veneer and each has two chairs of the vinyl metal frame variety. There's the DJ booth on the left, basically a nook with a high counter. The DJ sits in shadow, lit only by the soft glow of a soundboard. She controls the stage lights as well, as I will learn.

The stage is long and wide against a mirrored wall. There is a brass pole at one end. Chairs line it in a single row against a low ledge for drinks. Two customers sit at the stage watching a dark-skinned girl with waist-length dreadlocks slowly gyrate. Her nipples are covered with crosses of black electrical tape. I stare while trying not to stare. She is beautiful, sensuous, under the lights flashing blue on her dark skin. Black lights line the stage, hidden under the lip at the edge, and they make her G-string glow electric pink.

"Come on." Sierra leads me through the tables and past the stage to a black door hidden in the shadows of a black wall. She opens it onto more blackness, but my eyes adjust and I see light spilling around a heavy curtain. We step into musty darkness between the door and the fabric and then on through into a long, narrow room.

Battered lockers line one wall and a wide counter runs opposite. Above the counter the wall is mirrored, tube fluorescents making the room very bright. At the opposite end of the room is another door, and the near wall opens into a tiny bathroom: toilet, rust-stained sink. The floor is thin grey carpet. It is a battered, shabby room but it is also fairly clean. The mirrors gleam spotlessly and the worn carpet is stain free. Dust coats the corners of the bathroom but the toilet is new and shining. The room smells of sweat and competing aromas of body spray. Some of the lockers spill swills of fabric and tangles of shoes with very high heels.

A girl with waist-length brown hair relines her eyes with black kohl. She glances at me in the mirror. "Fresh meat?" she asks Sierra, going back to her delicate work. She wears tiny black hot pants and nothing else. Her nipples are covered in silver glitter.

"I'm Desire," I say, the name still unfamiliar on my tongue.

"Yeah, you are." She turns away disinterestedly.

"You can put your stuff here," Sierra says and opens a locker. A child's clothes hanger falls from the rod at the top with a clatter. "And you can put your makeup here next to mine." She scoots over a Caboodles makeup case to create a little more space on the counter. I set my case next to hers and sit down on one of the straight-backed chairs. I am not nervous, exactly.

Sierra pulls her shirt off and unclasps her bra with brisk efficiency. "Let me help with the pasties." She opens her kit and removes an adhesive bra. It is made from basically the same material as Band-Aids and comes in a variety of skin tones.

Laws governing public nudity vary from state to state. In this state women cannot show the pubic region, pubic hair, or nipples in public. G-strings and shaving or waxing take care of the lower bits and a variety of adhesives are used on the top. Tape, thick glitter paint, glue-on pasties, and adhesive bras are all used. Sierra explains to me that men like to think that they're seeing the real deal and thus she finds the adhesive bra is best because it looks natural from a distance.

"Let me see your nips," she instructs and I pull my shirt off. Her glance is clinical. The other women in the room glance, too, checking out the goods, then return to whatever they are doing.

"Same size as mine." She removes a circle of cardboard from her case and uses it as a stencil to cut four rounds of the adhesive with small scissors. She then slices along the radius. "Like this," she shows me, creating a cone shape by overlapping the radial edges. Removing the backing to expose the sticky, she pinches her nipple to make it erect. Then she expertly sticks the adhesive over her nipple in a small cone, creating the illusion of bare flesh. "Now watch." She removes a compact of powder that exactly matches the tan adhesive and brushes it over the edges of the tape, blending it with her skin. "Now you."

I go more slowly but manage to replicate her technique. My skin is lighter but the tan tape looks natural enough. I blend a bit of concealer along the edges.

Sierra has stripped off the rest of her clothes and stands naked before the mirror. The light is brutally bright. She looks her body over carefully, tweezing a stray underarm hair and popping a small whitehead on her shoulder. She covers the red mark with a dab of concealer.

I take a deep breath and remove the rest of my clothing, folding it to fit in the bottom of my locker. I pull on the velvet thong and zip up the black and white dress.

"You need to get a T-bar," Sierra says.

"A what?"

She pulls a scrap of fabric out of her locker. It's smaller than any G-string I've seen. She holds it up. "T-bar."

I learn that a T-bar is named because of the shape it makes in the back: a T of straps around the hips and between the legs. Strippers layer them to create different colors that glow in the lights and wear them as a second set of undies to ensure that nothing pops out. They're also worn so that a girl can strip off the top set of underwear during a private dance, adding to the illusion that she's showing more.

I jump when a curtain between two sets of lockers flies back and the beautiful black girl who had been on stage steps into the room. I hadn't realized that the entrance to the stage opens directly into the dressing room. The girl with long brown hair leaves through the curtain and I hear hands clapping.

The new arrival appraises me with jet eyes. "Look at the baby stripper shoes," she says with a laugh.

I flush, though there is no maliciousness in her voice. The sandals I hold in my hands look like church shoes compared to the 7-inch pink platforms strapped to the other girl's feet. They match her G-string. *T-bar*, I mentally correct myself.

Sierra takes no notice. "You ready?" she asks me.

I strap on my shoes. "Yes."

We exit back into the club and Sierra leads me to the DJ booth.

On duty is a woman who appears to be in her forties, her hair, bleached within an inch of its life, piled in complicated rockabilly whorls on top of her head.

"She's auditioning." Sierra jerks her chin at me.

The DJ looks at me over the top of her clipboard. "What's your name, honey?"

"Desire."

"What kind of music do you like?"

I list off a bunch of bands, mostly of the goth/industrial/dance variety. She nods.

She writes down my name on her clipboard and then adds Sierra's name underneath. "You're up after Heaven."

"Who's Heaven?" I ask.

"Her." She points at the girl with the long brown hair on stage.

"Okay." Still I feel no nervousness, only the tightness of excitement. I see the bills appearing along the stage as Heaven dances. "I'm gonna sit and watch."

Sierra shrugs and leaves me at a table, making her way to the bar where she greets the men there more extensively with hugs and smiles.

I watch Heaven dance. The music is heavy and fast but she moves slowly, her hips keeping the beat while the rest of her moves languidly. She is petals floating on a fast-moving stream. One part of her always keeps the beat: a tapping toe, snapping fingers, pulsing posterior. I see how she uses the music to create a sensual counterpoint of stillness against movement.

I look at her body with a critical eye. She is not perfect like in a magazine, I see with relief. A bit of cellulite on her ass that dimples when she flexes, and she's a bit thick through the waist. Her breasts hang heavy and full. I think that she's gorgeous but she is not airbrushed. She just looks like a young, human female. Judging by the bills bulging in her underwear—T-bar, I correct myself—the men think she's hot, too.

I can do this, I think and feel a thrill of elation. As Heaven's second song winds down I go backstage and step into the shadowed recess between the curtain and the stage. I feel my heartbeat pulsing in my chest. My skin begins to tingle.

"Good luck, new girl," Heaven says, breezing past me in a cloud of floral scent.

I recognize the song immediately and let the music build toward the opening crescendo before stepping out, taking a cue from Heaven and moving slowly, only my footsteps in time with the beat. I want to unleash every part of my body, but I keep myself in check, knowing that if I let the music take me I will only be frenetic, not sexy. This is not a dance club. This is a strip joint. And I am a stripper.

Three men sit along the stage and four more watch from the first row of tables. I ignore them for the moment, facing the mirrored wall at the back of the stage, admiring the way the black lights make the white dress glow, lighting my skin with purple. My blond hair, hanging in curls past my shoulders, catches the overhead lights in staccato pulses of red and green.

Slowly, only my head moving to the music, I lean forward toward the glass and my reflection. I am doubled, Desire times two. The short dress rides up on my thighs, revealing the thin strip of black fabric hiding my vulva. I smile and the girl in the mirror smiles back, all red lips and tumbling curls. It feels taboo, forbidden, exciting.

I turn my back on the mirror and slide down it, keeping my feet flat on the floor and my knees together. When my butt hits the stage, I pop my knees apart, flashing that thin strip of fabric. Dollars appear on the tip rail.

I lean forward into a crawl and slink toward the first customer. He tips his head back to see me more clearly, the bill of his baseball cap shadowing his face. All I can see is the glitter of his eyes.

"Now on stage one!" The DJ's voice booms through the

sound system. "Desire." She draws my name out into a hiss. "Auditioning right now, she's never danced before! Come see her naked for the very first time."

I feel a twinge of irritation at the attention called to this being my first time on stage. It makes me more nervous. But two of the men sitting at tables get up and take seats at the stage. Apparently watching a woman take her clothes off "for the very first time" has appeal. I flash on the references to "fresh meat." Men seeing a woman naked for the first time is analogous to the value placed on female virginity. In our puritanical culture, sexuality pollutes a woman and we love nothing so much as to see her dirtied.

These thoughts do not show on my face. I smile slightly at the man in the baseball cap and put my knees on the padded tip rail, stretching my arms over my head. Slowly I run the zipper on the front of the dress down, revealing the bikini top I wear underneath. His eyes skim down my body hungrily. Mimicking what I had watched Heaven do, I pull out the strap of my G-string. He places the dollar into the strap, careful not to touch my skin. This club is strictly no touching and he knows the rules.

"Thank you," I mouth at him and move along the tip rail to the next customer, still on hands and knees. I stretch out on my back in front of him, feet on the floor. From this new vantage point I see up past the lights into rafters. The dropped ceiling stops at the stage, and the lights are fixed to metal girders attached to the roof. The pole on the stage rises past the sight line of someone sitting in the first row and is also attached to the roof beams. The wall above the mirrors along the back of the stage is painted black and so are the rafters and ceiling beyond so it all just looks like shadow. But from stage I can see it all. This place is illusion and I wonder if I will become unreal.

I gyrate my hips slowly and the customer watches my belly undulate. "You're beautiful," he says, and I hold out the strap for his dollar.

The first song blends into the second. It's time to take my top off. I stand, back to the audience, facing myself in the mirrors. The black lights that line the tip rail glow purple on the long stretch of my legs, and the lights above flash off my hair and skin. I reach up and slowly pull the tie of my bikini top. The men shift forward in their seats. I let the top drop, keeping one arm across my breasts. This is not due to anxiety; I'm only heightening the anticipation. It works: more money appears on the stage.

I pivot suddenly and lift my arms over my head. Now I'm wearing only the G-string and shoes. And the pasties, of course.

Being (mostly) naked does not feel particularly strange to me. I love being naked. Making money off of it seems ludicrously easy.

I slink along the rail in time to the beat, bending over, preening, bouncing my breasts, taking the money. It's exciting and I let the beat take me, actually dancing for a moment. More money appears.

At the end of the set, my underwear bulges with dollars. As the music ends and the DJ's voice announces the next dancer, I pick up my discarded clothes and push back through the curtain into the dressing room.

"How'd it go?" Sierra asks.

"Fine," I say, retying my top and setting the pile of money carefully before my things.

"How much did you make?"

"Um...maybe $20? I lost count." I begin to straighten the money.

"Make sure all the bills face the same way," Sierra instructs.

"Okay. Why?" I ask.

"The club will buy back the ones at the end of the night, but they all have to be faced the same way."

"Oh." I start organizing the bills and she reaches to help. I have made $22 my first set. I quickly calculate that two sets an hour equal about $40 an hour, vastly more money than most other jobs.

I make enough on stage that first night to buy my first pair of big girl shoes. I choose studded heels in soft black leather with straps that crisscross over the top of my foot. The bottom two inches of the heels are metal that catches the lights of the stage, winking dangerously.

I pick up three shifts a week, on average making $150 a night. I begin conducting all my transactions in cash. When I switch clubs a year and a half later, after graduating from college, the money more than doubles. I don't feel unreal at all.

Chapter Two

Stripper Barbie

I am plastic, fantastic porn. I lie on my back in the middle of the stage, watching myself in the mirror on the ceiling. I have no idea why there's a mirror on the ceiling; it's recessed behind the stage lights, out of the sight line of people sitting at the stage. I am a voyeur, spying on myself.

On my back my hipbones jut, pulling taut the fabric of my red T-bar, creating a seductive cave of shadow over my pubis. Like so many things in this business, one can *almost* see the forbidden. The T-bar is much smaller than the bikini I wear in the sun, and thus my crotch and breasts glow paler than my golden skin.

"You're beautiful," the man sitting at stage says.

"Thank you," I reply.

It's rote now, this acknowledgment of admiration. I hardly notice.

Girls in American society suffer a frightening loss of self-esteem at puberty, and I had been no different. It didn't help that I lived in a small town with small minds. In middle school I became the target of intense bullying. It got so bad that my parents moved temporarily so that I could change schools. The hit on my self-worth felt permanent.

In the mirror I watch the lights play across my body: red, blue, a pulse of green. My blond hair, splayed out in curls on the black Formica of the stage, looks serpentine, Medusa-like.

High school and college helped tremendously. I had a series of friends and romantic partners who helped me repair myself, rebuild. Stripping completed that process.

Real women who strip are not what is found on television or in the movies. Over the course of my career, I worked with women of all shapes and sizes and colors. Girls with bad skin perfected makeup to rival Hollywood artists. Girls with stretch marks wore G-strings that came up higher, hiding the imperfection. We employed numerous tricks to conform to the ideal beauty standards, but the veneration of countless customers is what really did the trick for me. The flashing lights of the stage did not entirely hide imperfections of the skin, thick thighs, boney feet. The customers who plied us with cash and compliments recognized our humanity and adored us anyway.

I worked with two women, Celeste and Trinity, who had very similar body types. Both were white, thin, and small breasted. Celeste was a brunette and Trinity a blond, but otherwise they looked quite a bit alike. Trinity had a son and the impact that the pregnancy had on her body caused her no small amount of anxiety. She worried about her small breasts: that they weren't good enough. The stretch marks on her belly did not tan to the same golden as the rest of her skin.

Celeste had no such anxieties. She loved referring to her "mosquito bites" and would pinch her nipples to make them stand up proudly. She had stretch marks along her thighs, caused by a sudden growth spurt during puberty, and she joked about having them tattooed in, like tiger stripes.

These two girls were equally popular. They both had regulars and made good money. But Trinity had low self-esteem while Celeste did not.

Trinity and I share a regular so the two of us often find ourselves together. Our regular, a mild-mannered bachelor for life, brings us dinner every Wednesday and the conversation often strays into the personal. Trinity confides in the two of us that another of her regulars had offered to pay for breast augmentation.

"What?" I exclaim. "You can't do that!" The idea of a man paying to alter my body horrifies me on a visceral level. It feels like ownership, invasive and controlling.

"You're perfect the way you are," Paul agrees without

hesitation. "Big boobs aren't everything."

Trinity looks taken aback. She's expecting us to congratulate her, to be pleased that one of her regulars cared for her enough to drop this kind of cash for her happiness.

"I've always wanted bigger boobs," she explains. "I don't feel like a woman. I feel like a little girl."

"Um, I think you're all woman," Paul offers.

"Look at Celeste," I venture. "I don't think she feels like a little girl." I point to the stage where Celeste lay on her back with her legs wrapped around a customer's shoulders, her crotch, covered in a thin layer of tropical fabric that glowed in the black lights, inches from his face. He says something, grinning, and she laughs, her head thrown back.

"She hasn't had a kid," Trinity retorts.

"So?" I shoot back. "The only reason anyone knows that you have a kid is because you tell everyone!"

She looks at me, solemn. "You wouldn't understand." Her gaze drops to my chest, the swelling rise of my breasts under a black bikini top.

"It's not like I'm huge!" I retort.

"But your clothes fit."

"What are you talking about?"

She gestures at her own flat chest. "Everything just hangs on me."

"So what?" I can't seem to say anything else. I just cannot understand. "You always look adorable. Athletic."

She crosses her arms self-consciously. "I'm getting them."

Paul and I look at one another helplessly.

"They're gonna look fake," I say.

"I don't care," she replies.

Strippers can spot fake tits at 500 yards. I only met one pair of boobs that I didn't know were fake. Tiana worked with me for a couple of years. A big-boned blond Russian, she sported huge swelling breasts that bounced becomingly on stage. They moved naturally with her body, including the big test: when she lay on her back, they fell normally to the sides.

One day she let slip that she had augmented them before coming to the United States. "What?" I exclaimed, disbelieving. "No way."

"Feel." She placed my hand on her left breast.

I squeezed carefully, feeling just the resistance of flesh. Fake usually feels too firm, sometimes even hard. It's often possible to feel the implant itself if it has been inserted over the muscle. Implants inserted behind the muscle are better but more expensive. And they still usually feel rigid.

"Amazing," I said appreciatively.

"Expensive," she grinned.

Now, I ask Trinity, "Are you going over the muscle or behind?"

"My regular is putting up $3000. But I'm gonna pay the extra two grand and have the implants put behind the muscle."

"Longer recovery time," I say. Paul's head turns between the two of us like in a tennis match. I want to laugh but don't.

"I'll be out a month."

"I wish you could just be happy with who you are," I say. Paul nods in agreement.

"I will be," Trinity says.

I throw up my hands.

She's out for a month. When she returns, her tank top fits much differently. Her new breasts look good: no scarring, perfectly symmetrical placement, big but she didn't overdo it. To a trained eye they're obviously fake but they look nice, overall. Paul tells her that she looks beautiful and she beams with pleasure.

In the dressing room I ask her about the procedure.

"Oh, my god!" she exclaims dramatically. "It hurt so bad for the first three days! I thought I had made a huge mistake."

"Didn't you have painkillers?"

"Yes, but it still *hurt*. And everything was bruised and horrible looking. But then it all started to heal. And now I love them!" She laughs.

Over the next few days I watch as her confidence blossoms. She has always been an outgoing and ebullient girl but now she positively radiates. Her mood translates into tips and her income soars.

All I feel is conflict: I can't argue with the results. She's happy, confident. She thinks that she's making more money because of the implants, but I suspect that it's because of her newfound confidence in herself.

Why must a woman's sense of her own value be so deeply tied to her physical appearance? Specifically, why does our culture sexualize breasts to the point that augmentation is the most common invasive cosmetic procedure in this country? Our culture sexualizes breasts, which makes men focus on them, which makes women obsess over them, which creates an industry that profits off of women's insecurity, which drives our national obsession. It's a horribly vicious cycle.

It's also not uncommon to have customers offer to pay for various augmentations. It's a way to establish ownership over a woman's body, to make her conform to a fantasy. To a woman with low self-esteem the temptation to "correct" perceived imperfections can be almost impossible to ignore.

For me, the adulation far outweighed the criticism. Supportive friends and thoughtful lovers started my healing process. A parade of strangers worshipping at my feet finished the process. I never augmented my body to get more acclaim. I found myself. Trinity lost part of herself.

Chapter Three

A Bad Night

My schedule has become almost completely nocturnal. I'm in the last stages of completion of my master's thesis on vampires as religious archetypes, so I suppose it's fitting. On the nights that I don't work I sit in front of my computer, open books scattered across my desk and the floor, writing sometimes until dawn streaks the sky. I'm getting enough sleep, but my stress level is high and I'm probably drinking a little too much. The only exercise I get is at work and my skin has become so pale it's translucent.

I arrive for work later than normal and I haven't done my hair. I leave my curling iron on and check in for my first dance with my hair piled on top of my head in an unruly mop. The general manager comes over to my stage and tells me to tidy up my appearance.

"I know," I snap at him. "I'm just running a little late today."

He glowers at my sharp response. I haven't been working in this club very long and I haven't earned the right to talk back.

"There's no one in the club anyway," I point out.

He points a stubby finger at me. "Get your shit together, girl," he says, and stomps off.

I get off stage without making a single dollar. Like I said, the club is dead this early. There's only one stage open and the regulars sit at the bar, eyeballing me for free. The tables on the floor are empty.

I sit down at the counter in the dressing room and go to work on my hair. It gets frizzy in this climate and I tame it into ringlets. Twenty minutes later I'm looking more or less like myself.

When I return to stage there's a single customer sitting at the end with his back to the bar. He's an old dude in a sweat-stained tank top and gym shorts. He looks like he just crawled out of a culvert, but the club is in an area where sometimes millionaires look like gutter trash. I slink toward him.

It takes me a minute to recognize the long, thin shape hanging from his shorts for what it is. He sees the recognition on my face and spreads his legs wider, pulling up the waist of his shorts with one hand. The other hand lays a dollar on the stage. The shape dangles.

I shudder in revulsion. I ignore the dollar and stomp my foot down hard on the stage to get Damon's attention. The bouncer looks up at me and I tilt my head, beckoning.

Damon hurries over.

"The dude at the end of the stage has his penis hanging out of his shorts," I say.

Damon's eyes widen as his head turns sharply to look. Old dude grins at him, too, not even trying to hide.

"What the..." Damon walks over and lays one firm hand on old dude's shoulder. "Come on, buddy, you're outta here."

When the man stands his shorts ride up even further, revealing greying pubic hair and one testicle. I look away.

"Cover yourself up or I'll have you arrested," Damon barks.

"But isn't that what these bitches are for?" old dude whines.

Damon hauls him to the exit, none too gently. "Get the fuck out." He pushes hard enough that the guy stumbles. "And don't come back."

I leave the dollar on the stage. That's zero for two sets. Lovely. I head to the smokers' lounge to see if anyone is back there playing pool. I want someone to buy me a drink and talk to me like a normal person.

Sadie and Veronica are the only people in the smoking room. Sadie pulls up a chair and offers me a cigarette.

"I just had some homeless-looking guy flash me his dick," I inform them.

"Ewwww!" "Gross!" they say in tandem.

"Why do men think we want to see that shit?" Veronica asks

rhetorically.

"Maybe he was just some old pervert," I say. "Mentally ill."

"Or maybe he can only get off by forcing women to look at his junk," Sadie counters.

I shudder, but a crowd of guys comes in at that moment and we all straighten. It turns out that they're good for a round of drinks. The DJ opens the stage in the smoking lounge.

Several songs later I take the stage. One of the guys comes over with a handful of dollars. I crawl across toward him and catch the silver stud through my tongue between my teeth. Flicking my tongue makes the stud dart like a snake, clicking rhythmically against my teeth. He watches the metal flash, hypnotized.

"What else you got pierced?" he asks.

I just laugh, letting him wonder.

"I have a Jacob's ladder," he says.

"What's that?" I ask naively.

Before I even know what's happening, he turns his back on me, drops his trousers, and bends over. More piercings than I can count at a glance run from the base of his testicles all the way up the shaft of his penis.

I gasp in surprise.

"Bet that would feel good," he says pulling up his pants.

"I can't imagine," I say weakly, pulling the strap of my G-string out for the dollars.

At the end of my set I storm to the dressing room and throw my purse down on the counter. "That's two penises I've seen tonight," I tell Blake. "Count them. Two."

"What?" she exclaims.

I brief her on the events of my first hour at work. She gapes at me, laughing in amazement.

"I can't wait to see what my third set will bring!" I say.

I decide to wait in the dressing room. I've had enough of the floor for a while, and so I sculpt elaborate eye makeup and redo my hair.

I'm called to stage one and my mood lifts when I hear the familiar strains of my music. There's a group of five guys sitting at stage. They all have drinks in front of them and piles of bills all waiting and ready to go. Maybe this night will turn out okay.

They tip moderately and I warm up into my second song. I kneel on the tip rail and take my top off, bouncing my breasts provocatively.

The guy in front of me watches with a noncommittal expression and doesn't put up a dollar. I don't let my expression change.

Then he leans toward me. "How old are you?" he asks.

I hesitate. It's an unusual question. I get asked all kinds of things but I've never been asked my age before.

"Twenty-two," I tell him.

He looks amused. "No, how old are you really?"

I look at him uncertainly. "I'm 22," I say again.

"You sure you're not more like 35?"

I'm dumbfounded. I make it a point not to care about age, but more than ten years older than I actually am is startling.

"What, do you want to see my fucking driver's license?" I snarl.

He puts his hands in the air mollifyingly. "Are you really 22?"

"*Yes*," I insist.

He shakes his head at me. "Well. You're looking a bit rough around the edges."

All I can do is glare at him, speechless.

He holds his hand out. "Sorry. Let's start over. Friends?"

I shake his hand, not knowing what other action to take. I finish the set but he never tips me. Neither do his friends. I make a measly $6.

In the dressing room I look at my face critically. I admit that I look tired. I've been pushing myself hard, and the pressure shows in the shadows under my eyes and the fine lines around my mouth.

"What are you looking for?" Blake asks, watching my self-assessment.

"Some dude just refused to believe that I'm 22," I tell her. "He insisted that I look 35."

She gives me a dangerous look. "I'm 34."

I bite back irritation. "I'm not saying that people in their thirties don't look good," I explain. "Or forties. Or whatever. I'm just..." I trail off. I don't know what I am.

"You're just having a weird night," she fills in. "And dudes think young is hot."

"Yes," I sigh. "I am definitely having a weird night."

"Don't let it get to you." She pats my shoulder. "Remember: these guys don't define you."

I nod. "Thank you," I say. "Dudes are assholes."

She smiles at me. "I hear that."

I pat concealer under my eyes and head back onto the floor. For some reason none of my regulars are showing tonight. I really need some friendly conversation, some normalcy, but it's nowhere in sight. I head over and stand next to the bar, surveying the club. It's filling up but none of the faces are familiar. It's become a strange, hostile place. I feel anxiety well up in my stomach and I take a deep breath. I spot a nice-looking guy sitting alone at a table in the middle of the floor. I force myself to make my way over to him.

"Hi," I say when he looks up. "I'm Natasha."

He smiles at me. "Hi, yourself," he says. "I'm Walt. Would you like to sit?"

I smile back. "I'd love to." I slide into the seat next to him. "Are you having a good night?" I feel the tight knot in my middle loosen a little.

"It's better now."

I widen my smile at him as the waitress makes her way over. Finally, the hope of a drink.

"Would you like something?" he asks and I gratefully accept, ordering a full-strength cocktail. Sometimes a little self-medication is totally in order.

"I love your look," he says after we've placed our order.

"Thank you," I reply. I'm wearing my favorite outfit. It's all studs and spikes and leather.

"How many piercings do you have?" he asks.

I flick my tongue stud at him.

"Anything else?" His eyes wander lower.

I shrug, smiling slightly. I get asked this all the time. Men are wild to know if I have genital piercings and I always demur, letting them wonder and make their own assumptions.

He hikes his shirt up, revealing a pale chest. In each nipple is a large-gauge ring, the weight pulling against his flesh in a way that I find revolting. But I grin enthusiastically. "Nice!"

"Do you have yours done?" he asks.

"I do not," I reply carefully. "My nipples are very sensitive. I'm afraid of losing sensitivity if I pierce them."

"You should gain sensitivity."

I laugh. "That might be worse! They're sensitive enough as it is."

Our drinks arrive and I take a long sip. The alcohol warms its way down my throat. "Would you like a private dance?" I ask.

To my relief Walt says yes without hesitation and I lead him into the private area. He watches appreciatively as I go into my routine.

I lean into him, my breath along his neck.

"Bite me," he whispers.

I pull away slightly. "What?"

He looks into my eyes. "I want you to bite me. Hard."

I look into the mirrored wall behind him, relieved to see Derek the bouncer watching the private area. Doing his job. I can use him as an excuse not to sink my teeth into this stranger's flesh.

"I'll get in trouble," I whisper back, biting my lip, letting him see my teeth. His gaze homes in on my mouth. I pull away from him and lean into the mirror. Touching him creeps me out.

He rests his hand on the stage. "Step on my hand."

I look at him over my shoulder. "You like pain?"

"Oh, yes," he moans.

This I can do. I place the ball of my foot on the back of his hand and apply firm downward pressure.

"Harder," he whispers and I shift my weight forward, feeling the bones in his hand flex under my foot. It feels very strange but, given the night I'm having, a small tingle of pleasure erupts in my brain. It feels kind of good to hurt someone.

I press down until he gives a gasp of pain, and then relent. He holds his hand to his chest, rubbing it vigorously. At the end of the song he tips me an extra ten.

"Can I ask you a question?" he asks me as I'm pulling my clothes back on.

"Sure," I say, feeling a drop in my stomach.

"Will you pierce my dick?"

"What?" I exclaim, pausing in pulling my skirt on.

"I'll pay you," he rushes to explain. As though that is the problem.

"You want me to put a needle through your penis," I say for clarification.

"Yes, please." His eyes are too bright, shining with excitement.

I finish pulling my clothes on and sit on the edge of the stage. I take his hand, the injured one, in mine. His breath quickens. "I can't do that," I tell him.

"I'll give you a grand," he says.

For a moment I consider it. That's a lot of money.

"*No,*" I insist when my sanity returns. "The only thing I've ever pierced is my own ears. There are nerves. And blood vessels. I could really hurt you."

"I don't care."

"No," I say again, standing up. "I can't." I walk away, feeling his eyes on me.

There's less than an hour left in the shift. I am nothing but relieved. I haven't even made a hundred dollars and it feels as though everyone I've talked to tonight has turned totally loony tunes. I go up for my final set on stage one. The customers there get up and leave. Of course. I'm beyond caring.

But here comes Walt. I sigh internally. I'd thought he'd left but he's clearly been lurking somewhere. He sits and puts up a five.

I slink toward him and sink into the splits, keeping my back to him. I roll forward, my butt in his face. Maybe if I can keep him from speaking to me.

In the mirror I see the general manager materialize over Walt's shoulder. I don't think anything of it; it's his job to patrol the floor. But then he wags a finger at me. I stand up and go to the edge of the stage, leaning down to hear him.

To my shock, he grabs me by the upper arm, hard. "You trying to get the club shut down?" he hisses.

"What?" I feel like I've been saying this a lot tonight.

"You have pubic hair showing."

I gape at him. It's against state law for a dancer to have a single hair show around her bottoms. We can dance topless, fully nude in clubs that don't serve alcohol, and yet a single hair can get the club fined or even closed for 30 days if there are multiple infractions. As a result, the dancers make grooming a priority.

"That's impossible," I tell him.

"Get your clothes on and get offstage," he snaps at me.

I don't say anything, just do as he tells me. I don't want to dance for creepy Walt anyway.

In the dressing room I sit in a chair and start pulling off my jewelry. I feel numb. Finally, I go stand before the full-length mirror and bend over, checking my crotch. No hair.

"What the fuck?" I say to myself.

Sadie overhears me. "What's up?"

"That weasel GM just told me that I was showing pubic hair."

"Oh, yeah," she says, not surprised. "He likes to do shit like that to the new girls."

"Why?" I ask.

She shrugs. "I don't know. Power trip? Show us he's in charge?"

This makes me feel marginally better. It's just hazing. That I can handle.

I start pulling off my clothes to change into my jeans and hoodie. I am ready to get out of here.

At home I snuggle into Greg's sleeping body. He's all warmth and soft skin. He wakes enough to slip his arms around me. I bury my face in his shoulder.

"What's the matter?" he asks, sleepy.

"I had a bad night," I tell him.

He kisses the top of my head. "It's over now," he tells me.

Chapter Four

Material Girl

"Let me take you shopping," Alo says.

I gaze at him coquettishly over the lip of my glass, taking slow sips to buy myself time. I don't like customers to buy me things; I'd much rather take their money. Cold, hard cash is this girl's best friend.

But a shopping trip is vastly preferable to being brought presents. Men insist on buying me gold, a metal that I never wear. I think it makes me look jaundiced. All my things are silver or platinum. Only a very few men have ever actually noticed. I am a cutout girl in their minds, a stereotype to dress and adorn.

I also only meet customers outside of the club under special circumstances. I am not stupid; I know that one out of three women in our country is sexually assaulted. I work in an industry that inherently objectifies women, and some of the men who visit clubs assume that they have bought the rights to whatever they want to take.

Alo isn't one of these men. He's in his early forties, never married, no kids. He makes really good money and spends it carefully. He shares a house with a brother, likewise a bachelor, and lives frugally. He spends his money on clothes, cars, and me. He tells me that he has an investment portfolio of five million and I believe him. He plans to work until he's 50 and then retire to someplace tropical.

He'd initially come to the club for a friend's birthday. But then he met me. He likes me, likes my intelligence, my humor, and yes, my body. But he's never tried to touch me; he's never propositioned me, or said a single disrespectful thing to me.

A few weeks earlier I had gone with him to get his first tattoo. In exchange, he paid for me to get my tongue pierced and a small tattoo on the back of my neck. He'd also let me drive his car, a 911 Carrera. On our outing he'd treated me with nothing but care, opening doors for me, buying me dinner and then laughing when I ordered a milkshake for my tender tongue. He never asked for my home address, agreeing to meet me in neutral locations. He never inquired about my personal life nor wanted to know if I had a boyfriend.

Perhaps sensing my hesitation, he says, "I need to pick out gifts for my sister and my mom. I need a woman's insight."

I gesture down at myself. "Are you sure you need help from this sort of woman?" I'm wearing a fire engine red velvet catsuit, spiked dog collar, and the signature silver rings that encase three of my fingers in metal.

Alo laughs, too. "I've seen you in the real world. I know you're capable of looking normal!"

I shrug and agree to meet him at the mall on Sunday.

I meet him at a restaurant and we have lunch before shopping. He's as polite as ever, telling me about adventures with his niece and nephew, fun tidbits from his job. He asks me about my studies and listens intently to my answers, asking intelligent questions. I'm relaxed with him. I like him and consider him a friend. Albeit a friend who pays hundreds of dollars to see me naked.

After lunch we hit the shops. I help him pick out a robe for his mom. In the sleepwear department he purchases the robe, and five bra and panty sets for me. After that we wander into the home section and I pick out a beautiful glass pitcher for his sister. After, he suggests a stroll through clothing and he buys me a beautiful black lacy skirt, motorcycle boots, and a silver velvet top. In jewelry he buys me a silver choker with tiny diamonds.

"While we're here I should pick up some shirts," he says. "Do you mind?"

"Of course not!" I reply. "Where do you want to go for those?"

He names a high-end men's store at the other end of the mall.

I offer to carry some of the bags but he refuses. We walk slowly, admiring the holiday decorations on display, and window shopping as we go.

In the window of a furniture store I spot a coffee table that stops me in my tracks. It is unlike anything I own. It has a white faux marble base and a glass top. It is simple, elegant, and striking.

"Look at this!" I exclaim. "That is a totally cool coffee table."

"It is," Alo agrees. "Do you want it?"

I look at him doubtfully. "You want to buy me a coffee table?"

"Why not?"

"Um..." I bend down so that I can see the price. "It costs $800!"

"So?"

I look back at the table. It is beautiful. I want the *money* but I know he'll never just give me that amount. For some reason many of the men I meet in the clubs want to give me things as opposed to money. Maybe it makes them feel as though I'm a girlfriend. It lets them forget that our relationship is primarily a financial transaction. Alo gives me about a hundred dollars a night two nights a week. I'll never get eight bills out of him all at once.

I don't need an $800 coffee table. But I kind of want it.

"You really want to buy me this table."

He shrugs. "If you want it."

I think about how it would look sitting at the foot of my bed. It would make my bedroom look like a castle. "I think I do." I look at him carefully. I want to make sure there are no strings attached. His expression is the same as always: gentle and benign.

"It's a neat table," he says. "I think you should have it."

"Okay," I finally agree. "I've never had anyone buy me a table before."

He smiles. "First time for everything."

Inside, he pays in cash. He always pays in cash. I'm not even sure he has a bank account. When the clerk asks how we plan to take the table I look at him, startled.

"That won't fit in the car," I say, surprised that this detail hasn't occurred to me.

"We can deliver it," the clerk says helpfully.

Alo nods. "We'll do that. Give them your address and you can work out the details."

I hesitate as the thought crosses my mind that he's about to learn where I live.

"I'll be down looking at shirts," he says, smiling at me. "Meet me there?"

I don't know if he's anticipated my concern or if he really is interested in getting to his shirts. Either way, it solves my problem.

"Sure thing," I reply. "I'll be down in a minute."

I make the arrangements and then go help him buy shirts. He's picky about the fabric and fit but less so about the color and pattern. I help with this detail, advising him on things that will bring out the golden hue of his complexion.

Afterward, on the way back to the car, he hands me the car keys. I like drive, the acceleration, the control. This car is so responsive it's like it can read my mind. I take the keys eagerly.

The coffee table is delivered two days later. I position it at the foot of my bed and stand back to admire the effect. I'd thought about returning it and taking the cash. It comes with the receipt and he'd paid in cash. I could have gotten the money.

But I'm right: at the foot of my black iron bedframe it looks awesome. I arrange ivory candles in black holders along it and light them, filling the room with flickering light. I decide to keep the table.

Chapter Five

Body Property

I'm on stage two and the club is packed. It's about 11 p.m. on a Saturday and we're all making good money. There's a hum of laughter and conversation below the pounding music, and the air conditioner can barely keep up with the heat from active bodies. A light sheen of sweat covers my body.

At my stage every seat is taken. My G-string overflows with dollar bills. The corner seats are occupied by four men out celebrating something, a birthday maybe. I haven't yet been able to ascertain the nature of their visit, but they keep pushing one of their party forward, piling the ones in front of him.

I press into the mirror, slowly bending forward so that the V of fabric between my legs becomes visible. I've stripped to my shoes and underwear by this point in the set. I cross my legs at the ankles and sit suddenly, twisting so that now I'm facing my audience, knees up, legs crossed demurely. The crowd hollers.

Silkily I crawl across the stage toward the man with the pile of money before him. When I get to him I brace my knees on the padded lip that runs around the stage and kneel before him, breasts lifted, stomach taut. Slowly, I lift one leg until my toes rest on the pad, rotating my knee outward so that the fabric of my underwear pulls tight across my pubis. It's a move I've done hundreds of times and it gives the illusion that they're seeing more than they actually are. When I wear a black G-string over a bright one that catches the black lights the illusion is made stronger by the flash of brilliant, glowing color between my legs.

I can usually tell when someone is going to make a grab for me, but this dude moves too fast for me to catch. His hand darts between my legs and suddenly his fingers press into me, his thumb shoving into my flesh.

The only thing I'm aware of feeling is a blinding flash of rage that drowns out the music and the conversation. I react without thinking. I pick up the foot that rests against the pad edging the stage and stomp it down on his other hand, the non-offending one, that he's braced against the drink rail along the stage. I'm wearing my favorite shoes, the ones with the metal heels, and the thin spike slides through the webbing between his thumb and forefinger like butter.

I have not made a sound but he *screams*. I lean forward and grab his throat. I feel the tough flesh of his larynx cutting off his cry and I pull his face to mine. The hand between my legs is gone and I feel his fingers scrabbling around where my shoe has impaled him.

"Do not touch me!" I roar into his face. He whimpers and I look up, across the club, to where the bouncer is leaning casually against the bar. He hasn't yet noticed that anything is wrong.

"Paul!" I howl his name and my voice rises above the music.

He starts and then races toward me.

I feel a hand on my arm and I look down into the face of one of the other men, one of the friends. "Get your fucking hands off of me!" I snarl into his face and snap my teeth shut centimeters in front of his nose. He recoils.

"You bitch," the wounded man says weakly.

"You call me a bitch? You dare to touch me." I am so angry that I'm starting to shake and I twist my heel. He cries out again.

Now other people are finally starting to notice that something is awry. The other men at the stage gape and one of them starts to laugh, elbowing the man sitting next to him who starts to grin as well. The customers sitting along stage one begin to turn in their chairs, craning their necks to see. The dancer on stage one comes over to the edge of the stage and, from her elevated position, sees what's happening. She starts to laugh.

Paul reaches us. "Oh, my god," he says. Blood has begun to seep up around where my heel has the man pinned.

"He grabbed me," I explain in a growl. I still have him by the throat and now I push his head sharply backwards.

Paul grabs some napkins from a pile sitting next to the drinks that line the rail. He presses them around my heel. "Lift," he instructs me.

For a moment I do not comply, only stare at the man who assaulted me. There are tears in his eyes. I want to leap from the stage and tear into his face. One of his friends reaches for me again and this time it's Paul who slaps the man's hand.

"Don't touch her," he commands and at that I shift my weight back. I lift my shoe and Paul slides the man's hand down, off of my heel, pressing the napkins against the wound. "Hold that," he orders, and the man weakly wraps his uninjured hand around the pool of blood that darkens the napkins.

"What did he do?" Paul barks at me. Across the club I see the manager come around the bar and make his way toward us.

"He grabbed my crotch," I say to Paul, not taking my eyes off the face of the man. Mostly I see pain in his expression but there's anger as well. I'm not letting him out of my sight.

"What?" Paul exclaims.

Now it's not me but a man sitting farther along the stage who jumps in. "I saw it! He grabbed her, just like she said. His whole hand between her legs."

The whole club is watching now, but the DJ valiantly keeps up the schedule and announces the next dancer to stage. Sunny, the girl on stage one, leaves reluctantly, peering back over her shoulder the whole time.

Steve, the manager, reaches us. "Oh, my god!" he exclaims upon seeing the blood welling up around the napkins pressed to the man's hand. Turning on me, he demands, "What did you do?"

"He grabbed me so I put my heel through his hand," I explain. It seems rational to me.

"*What?*" Steve screams at me. It doesn't seem rational to him.

I feel his spittle spray on my face and I wipe my hand across my cheeks grimly. For some reason, every club I worked had some slimy little dude as the general manager. Their job is to make money but that often means treating the employees, especially the naked ones, as a means to an end. "Do not spit on me," I snarl at him.

Paul smoothly takes charge. He puts his arm between me and Steve and pushes the GM back. He's gentle but firm. "You," he addresses me. "Get dressed and meet me in the entrance. You," this is to Steve. "Get back behind the bar and let me handle this." He turns to the offending customer. "And you come with me." He hauls the man, much less gently, to his feet. His friends straggle along after.

The next girl to my stage stands on the steps watching. We're halfway into what should have been her first song. "Sorry," I say to her, gathering up my clothes and money.

She shrugs, grinning. "No worries."

"Thank you. I owe you." I pull on my top and skirt and hurry across to the entrance. It's a small alcove between the exterior and interior doors and consists of a small space with a cashier, a pay phone, and an ATM.

Mr Grabbypants is now yelling in Paul's face. "Call the cops! I'm gonna sue that bitch!" One of his friends takes a step toward the phone and another reaches toward his pocket where the top of a cell phone protrudes.

Paul is used to a variety of conflict situations and he never raises his voice. He merely reaches out and touches the wedding ring on the man's finger. "You want your wife finding out about this?" he asks in a soft, smooth voice.

"You call the cops and I'll have you charged with assault," I add.

"Assault," Paul repeats softly.

The two friends stop reaching for phones.

Mr Grabbypants will not be mollified. "You're just a whore,

bitch!" he screams at me. "Cops gonna believe you?"

The anger rushes back and I take a step forward. He flinches and I laugh. "You have no idea who I am," I tell him, my voice soft. He's lucid enough to hear the rage in my tone. "Yes, I am a stripper but I am a lot more than that. If you would like to find out more about who I am we can call the police right now. I have friends on the force." This is not a lie. The off-duty officers from the local precinct often drop by the club and I've become friendly with several of them. They patrol the streets around the club at closing time to make sure we're not followed when we leave the parking lot.

Paul lets go of his arm. "It's your call, man."

One of the friends steps forward. "Let's just go," he suggests.

"I recommend the hospital," I offer helpfully. "You need a tetanus shot."

Mr Grabbypants lets his friends lead him away. As the door closes he yells back over his shoulder, "You probably get off on hurting men. Perverted cunt."

I look at Paul. He smiles at me and I smile back. "What does that even mean?" I ask him. "Perverted?"

"It means whatever he wants it to mean." He opens the interior door, and the music and roar of conversation wash over us. "Let's go back inside."

Chapter Six

Fetish

I have pretty feet. They are thin and highly arched with long toes and even nails. The tendons ripple under the skin and the stripper shoes I wear make the vessels pulse. Unlike many of the girls, I mostly do not wear platforms. I prefer stilettos with 5-inch heels that reveal the top of my foot. I have the metal heels and bought the same pair in white. I have patent heels with an ankle strap, heels made of Lucite, and heels in red leather. Sometimes I wear boots as well. I own boots crisscrossed with silver buckles that come up over my ankles, knee-high go-go boots, and thigh-high vinyl boots with silver studs. Footwear is important because it's often the only thing on my body other than underwear. Strippers spend a lot on thongs and shoes.

The man is in his sixties, nicely dressed in tan pants and a striped dress shirt. He places a dollar on the stage and I squat before him, opening my knees provocatively. It is the first song of the set and I wear pleather pants that zip apart at the crotch, a tantalizing strip of silver teeth running between my legs. On top I wear a complicated vest of straps, a wide band across my breasts. I have paired the ensemble with the metal heels. His eyes never leave my feet.

The dollar secured in the elastic of my G-string, I move on to the next customer. It is early in the night but already six or seven men crowd my stage and the dollars pile up.

The older gentleman places a five on the stage. In reward for this generosity I stand with my back to him and slowly unzip the pants, revealing a neon green G-string that catches the black lights in an electric glow. He glances up appreciatively and then his gaze returns to my feet.

I spin to sit with my ankles crossed and slowly extend my

legs toward him. The pants, now detached in the middle, sag toward my knees and I push them down so that the cuffs cover my feet. He reaches out and pulls the garment off, caressing my ankle lightly as it is revealed.

This is technically a breach of etiquette. Customers are never allowed to touch us, though we can touch them as we wish. But I let it slide, putting one foot on either of his shoulders. Of course, this puts my glowing crotch directly in front of him but he turns his head to keep my foot in sight. He puts down another five-dollar bill.

Over the course of two songs, he's given me $30. With other tips I make almost $50 in less than ten minutes.

After my set I stop by his chair to thank him. Destiny is on stage, wearing silver heels with a 3-inch clear platform. He looks away from her and his eyes travel down my body.

"I'm Star," I say, holding my hand out to him.

His eyes travel back up to my face. "Gary. Very pleased to meet you."

"Let me know if you want to have a drink with me later."

He glances dismissively at Destiny. "How about now?"

I lead him to a table against the wall, conveniently located next to the private dance area. I catch the eye of a waitress and she makes her way over.

Some clubs pay dancers on the number of drinks they can sell, and the girls collect drink straws that they cash out at the end of the night. Some clubs dilute dancer drinks to keep their girls from getting too drunk. This club doesn't engage in either practice. Our drinks are served full strength and it's easy to have too many. So we have developed a system whereby the dancers signal to a waitress to bring them an alcohol-free drink while seeming to order one with booze.

"I'll have a Kim's Special," I tell her.

"What's that?" Gary asks.

"It's created by the bartender," I reply. "Very fruity. Tropical."

"What kind of alcohol?"

"Vodka."

If a customer orders one it actually does come with vodka.

"I'll have a gin and tonic," he tells the waitress.

I place my feet casually into his line of sight, crossing my ankles. "So, Gary. What brings you in tonight?"

"I'm in town for a conference," he replies. "It's a once-a-year type of thing. I didn't see you here last year."

"I just moved here a few months ago."

"You have beautiful feet," he says.

I arch my foot, pointing the toe. The tendons leap beneath my skin. "Thank you."

"May I?" He holds out a hand.

"Sure." I put my right foot into his palm. Gently he unclasps the buckle at my ankle and rubs his thumb across the line left by the strap. He does not remove my shoe. His hands are firm and dry and he handles me carefully, almost reverently.

"What size do you wear?"

"Nine," I tell him, hoping that he won't think this is too big.

He doesn't appear to react at all. "Will you give me a private dance?" he asks. "I'd like you to go barefoot."

"Of course." The possibility of taking off my shoes is actually delightful. My feet are used to heels but it still feels good to take them off.

Our drinks arrive and he takes a small sip.

"Shall we adjourn?" I ask, standing. We carry our drinks to the private dance area.

The private area consists of low, square stages about four by four. The customers sit in cushy armchairs. Each stage—there are four—is partitioned off by fake potted trees, creating small oases of privacy. Sometimes we drag up another chair for couples.

I set my drink on the corner of the stage and unbuckle the straps of my shoes, taking my time, making it part of the strip. Gary's eyes never leave my feet.

I pull off my outfit slowly until I stand nude except for the tiny G-string I wear. He doesn't even glance at the rest of my body.

"It's $20 a song," I tell him.

He lays four twenties on the edge of the stage.

It's a little disconcerting to dance naked for someone who is so focused on one body part. I'm used to having men stare; in fact, part of the point of clubs like this is allowing people to really look. Our society is puritanical with regard to sex, which is probably why we're so obsessed with it. Having the freedom to really look, see one another's bodies, can be profoundly liberating.

And titillating.

The other side of looking is being looked at. This is different than being seen: my friends and parents and lovers *see* me, who I am. My customers have my permission to look at me but sometimes they see me and sometimes they do not. Mostly, this is the service I sell: the freedom to look at my body, my breasts, my ass, my crotch, my skin, my hair.

And now my feet.

At the end of the four songs, Gary says, "If I bring you shoes, will you wear them?"

"Of course!" I say. "I love shoes."

"Don't all women love shoes?" he laughs.

I laugh as well.

"I'll be back in a bit."

"See you soon, then!"

I wonder where he plans to get shoes in my size at nine o'clock at night. There is an adult store in town but I'm not sure of the hours. Part of me wonders if I will see him again at all.

He's back an hour later with a box under his arm. I'm sitting chatting with a regular when he walks in. I catch his eye and he smiles. I smile back.

The shoes are brutal. They're my size but the heels are a full

6 inches with no platform. There is a bit of a cushion under the ball of my foot but my arch is held painfully bowed. They're also ugly: white snakeskin with a bit of silver detailing around the scales.

"Let me go change," I say. I'm wearing black and red and the shoes clash. "I have just the thing."

The shoes are better with a silver catsuit. It's one of my favorite outfits. There are skintight pants with a small bell at the ankle and a top with crisscrossed laces up the back. It makes me look as though I have been dipped in liquid metal.

As I slip the shoes back on after changing, I notice that they're lightly worn. These shoes are used. They have been on other feet. I don't think he bought them at all. I think he already *had* them. Which begs the question: does he travel with women's shoes in every size, passing them out as gifts to the pretty feet he meets?

Gary doesn't even really see the outfit. He's totally fixated on my feet. My feet, which are already aching.

"May I buy you off the list?" he asks.

"Yes," I say without hesitation. "Let me go tell the DJ."

It's relatively rare to have a customer buy a dancer off the list. The rate is $20 a song and the customer gets us all to himself. We can do private dances or he can just sit with us.

The DJ raises his eyebrows at me as he crosses my name off. "Have fun," he says.

I smack him on the shoulder. "You're just thinking about the big tip out you'll get."

He smacks me back. "Nope. Just about you in that silver outfit."

I roll my eyes. "Whatever."

"'*Whatever*,'" he mimics me. "You sound like a valley girl."

Luckily, Gary doesn't really expect me to stand in the ridiculous shoes he's brought. I spend most of the rest of the night lying on my back with my feet in his lap or on the arm of his chair.

I make $1200 that weekend. Then I don't see Gary for a year. I stash the shoes in the back of my locker and consider tossing them a couple of times. But I don't. A year later, the following summer, Alexandria bursts into the dressing room as I'm getting ready. "Star!" she exclaims. "Remember that foot guy?"

"Yes," I answer hesitantly.

"I think he's out there."

I can barely remember what he looks like. I approach without letting my hesitation show. But it's him. He returns every June for the years I work at this club. And I always have the shoes waiting.

Chapter Seven

Object of the Gaze I Become

The determining male gaze projects its phantasy on to the
female figure which is styled accordingly.
—Laura Mulvey

I became a stripper at the age of 19. I had just returned to the States
from spending time studying at the University of Oxford and I did
not want to live on campus in a dormitory. I wanted my own place
but could not afford it on the meager salary of my work-study
job. I also did not have time for a regular job, and minimum wage
was not much better than the work-study money I already made. I
needed a job that paid a lot and had flexible hours.

A friend had been working at a local club and I knew she
made a lot of money while keeping up with her classes. I have
no problem with modesty and so I decided to give it a try. I
ended up working for five years, quitting only after I graduated
with my master's degree. Working in this industry for as long
as I did illuminated the tensions and contradictions of being a
woman in a patriarchal culture. Patriarchal attitudes, reinforced
by our recent Victorian past, continue to inform perceptions
of female sexuality and the sexuality of women of different
racial backgrounds, and affect women's safety, self-esteem, and
confidence. The lessons I learned inside the clubs have stayed
with me, continuing to inform how I teach, what kind of a
feminist I am, and how I understand my position as a daughter,
wife, (female) professor, and woman.

American culture is permeated by the legacy of puritanical
Victorian attitudes. Sex workers are stigmatized and sometimes
also feel guilt arising from self-judgment. In their article "Women
and Health," authors Eleanor Maticka-Tyndale, Jacqueline

Lewis, Jocalyn P. Clark, Jennifer Zubick, and Shelley Young write:

> Women's sexual role is to attract, entice and sexually arouse men. This is precisely how exotic dancers describe their work. Women's gender role, however, prescribes relative passivity, with active initiation of physical contact ascribed to the male. In addition, sexual interaction is prescribed, particularly for women, as private, intimate, monogamous, and non-commercial. Thus, while women engaged in sexual labor may not be violating the female sexual role, they are violating their gender role. This produces an outcast status, with sex workers stigmatized and labeled as indecent, immoral, or "bad girls" (88).

Gender roles reinforce the impression that "good" women don't take their clothes off for money. When confronted by someone who breaks these norms we ask, "What kind of woman dances for money?...We assume she is not very bright, sleeps with her clients, and has a surplus of predatory, sexual power. [Popular movies teach us that] a 'good' dancer actually hates dancing and only does it when driven by circumstances beyond her control" (Barton 585). Selling one's body, or permission to look at one's body, to the highest bidder breaks every sanction we place on female sexuality. I suspect it also confirms other assumptions that are harder to admit: the concern that women really do only pursue men for money, the fear that all women are whores: manipulative, lying, predatory. At the very least, we expect for women in this profession to not enjoy what they do. If they profess to find enjoyment in the job, we either dismiss them as irredeemable or assume that they are lying.

Andreas G. Philaretou, in the article "Female Exotic Dancers: Intrapersonal and Interpersonal Perspectives" (2006), summarizing the conclusions reached by almost 20 studies of exotic dancers, writes:

> The aforementioned studies point to several commonalities concerning the lives of [female exotic dancers] and their occupation. These include: (a) their low socioeconomic status and dysfunctional family backgrounds; (b) the considerable monetary payoff of the occupation compared to other low wage, low skill or high wage, high skill full-time jobs; (c) the exciting and interesting nature of the job compared to the drudgery of highly routinized, low self-directionless, low satisfaction mainstream occupations; (d) the temporary illusory feelings of female power experienced while on the job; (e) the sexual titillation experienced from engaging in consensual erotic dances in front of a cheering male audience; and (f) the companionship, social support, and fun times experienced with fellow co-workers (42).

Society assumes, first of all, that women who take their clothes off for money are people "whose prospects for economic well-being outside exotic dancing are limited" (Maticka-Tyndale et al. 103). In other words, they are the undereducated from low economic classes who recognize that they can take advantage of the fact that sex work is the only occupation in the world where women regularly earn more money than men. Studies also acknowledge that many women find aspects of the job fulfilling: they have fun, make friends, can drink on the job, and still have time to pursue other interests including families, hobbies, and education. However, a common assumption is that women in sex work are objectified and in an occupation that is beyond their control—consider the findings above that refer to the feelings of female power as "temporary" and "illusory." Sex workers, we assert, cannot *really* be empowered.

Sex work is defined as "a service to satisfy a sexual fantasy, produce sexual excitement or arousal, and/or provide sexual satisfaction to the customer" though the satisfaction may be delayed (Maticka-Tyndale et al. 88). The assumption is that a (female) dancer caters solely to the needs of the (male) client, subverting her own desires, and even her own personality, in order to fulfill the wishes of the client. Understood this way, stripping can only be viewed as degrading, dehumanizing work in that it reinforces the stereotype that women's sexual desires can never be found in revealing her body for money and that it is only men who pay for gratification of sexual fantasies.

One example of this subjugation is "customers purchasing various body technologies and giving them as 'gifts'" (Wesely 655). A "body technology" is a method of controlling the appearance through clothing, makeup, costuming, and cosmetic surgery. Wesely goes on to tell us, "By buying breast implants for a dancer...the customer takes control of the effort to reshape the woman's body in the fantasy image. At the same time, the women sometimes felt powerful when they convinced customers to pay for body technologies" (ibid). Read in this way, the male customer literally transforms the body of the sex worker as an object of his desire. The dancer fulfills her gender role by passively allowing her body to be modified and, from the position of the enslaved, finds gratification and fulfillment in the attentions of her master.

Another example of the dancer-as-object is that she exists in order to make the club money. Thus, dancers are often required to conform to expectations set by the (male) club owners and general managers. Some clubs set weight requirements or measurement requirements. Other clubs dictate what types of costumes the dancers are allowed to wear. It is not at all uncommon to dictate the shifts a woman can work based on her perceived marketability. Over my time as a dancer, I had owners and managers try to tell me the kinds of clothes I could wear, what type of music I could select, and which shifts I could work. I witnessed clubs limiting the number of women of color on a shift because "black women are not what 'bring in the money'" (Wesely 658). I never saw a club limit the number of white dancers on a shift.

Women in our culture are not only objectified for the color of our skin but also simply because we display secondary sex characteristics. Dancers often report fearing for their safety, because, "[t]oo frequently, customers are excited by strippers precisely because they occupy the role of the dirty slut in fantasies shaped by Madonna-whore dualities and other sexist notions about sexually available women" (Barton 591). Some customers assume that they are purchasing more than the right to look. I was always careful to work in safe clubs where customers who got out of hand would be expelled and even permanently banned, the parking lots were cleared before the staff left for the night, bouncers escorted us to our cars, and local police patrolled the area.

However, there's a lot more to the issue of safety than many of the studies recognize: strippers are not the only women who fear for their safety. The writers of the articles on stripping seem to assume that only women in sex work fear for their safety. But *all* women have this fear. I'm now a college professor and I still check the dark corners of parking garages.

Furthermore, the access I gained to higher-end clubs committed to keeping me safe is intertwined with my white skin, blue eyes, and blond hair. Privilege functions in the clubs just like it functions in society as a whole. White women feel safer.

My experiences are more nuanced than what many of the studies portray: "Missing from the literature…is any analysis of the temporal experience of stripping" (Barton 587). Moreover, "We cannot unpack the complexities of stripping without speaking with dancers themselves and letting their narratives drive our understanding" (Pilcher 522). Numerous articles note the importance of first-person narratives but are limited in scope: interviews are difficult to obtain, sample sizes are small, the number of clubs a researcher can feasibly visit is limited. Furthermore, the studies that do account for dancers' experiences focus mainly on life within the club. Therefore, we need for "researchers to ask more questions of exotic dancers, such as their perspective of their work and other aspects of their life style in relation to body objectification, relationship satisfaction, and self-esteem" (Downs, James, and Cowan 751).

My work is also limited. I am white, from a well-educated family, and I have substantial economic opportunities. However, I worked in the clubs for five years. While not officially an academic at the time, I was on my way to becoming one. My insights are based on informal ethnography, in that I had not taken a research methods class at the time. Thus, I join the ranks of other dancers who have written autobiographies. However, I was also receiving training as an academic while a stripper: I kept a journal and recorded my experiences and observations. I interacted with hundreds of dancers and many hundreds of customers. I worked in several clubs in different parts of the country. I have insights to offer for those who wish to really seek understanding of the taboo, complex, and enlightening world of exotic dancing.

Section II

The Dialectic of the Abyss

Narrative identity takes part in the story's movement, in the dialectic between order and disorder.
—Paul Ricoeur

Chapter Eight

Fast and Loud

Working holidays is a gamble. I stand at the bar, bored. It's going on 9 p.m. on July Fourth, just about the time fireworks will be starting, people in lawn chairs and on blankets, bottles of beer hidden in paper bags that do nothing to disguise them, barking dogs, screaming children.

I think back to the first fireworks I can remember. My mom and dad, standing pressed against the pedestrian rails along the Tennessee River, me lifted in my mom's arms to see. She had held me up high, above the pressing crowd, and the first burst of sparks had been accompanied by a mighty BOOM and then fire rained down toward me. The fact that it burned blue and purple did not even register. I opened my mouth and *screamed*. I remember how puzzled my mother had been, reassuring me that she would never place me in harm's way, *never*, but I remained unconvinced. It seemed as though we would all catch fire and burn to ashes.

Now I stand against the gleaming polish of the chest-high bar, leaned back on my elbows, surveying the empty club. Or mostly empty. A couple of the regulars sit at their normal table but they're not good for money, just passing the time. They come to drink beer and eyeball pretty girls, tipping a buck a set between the two of them just for the sake of appearances.

The club doesn't have that many dancers. We run a short staff on holidays, the normal number cut from 15 or 16 to barely half that. Two of the stages won't even open tonight; we just run one in the main section and the other in the smoking room.

For something to do I decide to change out of the outfit I've been wearing since shift change. In the dressing room, Sienna sits at the long counter that serves as the dressing table, her bare feet propped against the edge, deep in the pages of a book. The general manager explicitly forbids hanging out in the dressing room but a couple of the old-timers can get away with it. I'm still too new to risk the GM's wrath. Sienna is in her early thirties and she's been working at the club for more than five years. She's one of those perfectly beautiful women: long legs, narrow waist, firm B cups, long brunette hair. She doesn't draw crowds but her few regulars are loyal and wealthy. She has one coming in later, the only reason she's here on the Fourth. Until then, she'll read her book and dance her sets when she's called to stage.

I open my locker and pull out the outfit I've brought expressly for tonight, the only nod to patriotism I'm capable of making. The little red shorts are from another outfit, but tonight I pair them with a black tank top that I've modified with red glitter paint to read "think! it's patriotic" over an embossed American flag. I kick off the black stilettos I've been wearing and take my seat at the dressing table. If I fuss with my hair and makeup long enough, I can avoid the GM's watchful eye by claiming that I have a legitimate reason to be in the dressing room.

I carefully touch up the heavy black eyeliner I wear and then dot red glitter over my lids and cheekbones. Bright red lipstick completes the look.

Sienna glances at me over the top of her book. "You can't wear that," she says.

I glance down at my outfit defensively. "Why not?"

"Too political." Her nose buries in her book again. "Strippers aren't supposed to be political."

"Yeah, well if I'm going to work holiday shifts I'm gonna express myself," I retort.

"What? You think you're a person?" There is no animosity in her voice, just the matter-of-fact tone of a genuine question.

I grab the miniature lunchbox that serves as my purse. "I guess that depends on who you ask."

Her chuckle follows me out of the dressing room.

I stand at the top of the three steps leading up into our private area, leaning my arms against the railing while I survey the club. Destiny is on stage, her body stretched against one of the poles, pulsing in a gentle rhythm to the music. A couple of crumpled bills lie on the stage. She's doing the absolute minimum amount of work for the nonexistent crowd.

At the door I catch a glimpse of motion and amble over toward the bar for a closer look. A group of at least seven guys stand in line, money in hand, waiting as the doorman checks their identification and makes change for the cover. They're young, in their twenties, and while there is a certain amount of energetic conversation among them, they don't seem too rowdy.

On holidays sometimes groups come in completely wasted after partying elsewhere. Sometimes drunk crowds have loose wallets but mostly they're just troublemakers. These men show some promise.

I hear my name as the DJ calls me to stage. I make my way over and stand on the steps as Destiny gathers up her clothing and meager earnings.

"Group just came in," I tell her.

Her eyes light up. "Good deal," she says. "Maybe we'll actually make some cash."

"We'll see." I shrug as the first strains of my music come through the speakers. It's something by The Cure. The DJ knows how to play for me; early in the evening or when it's quiet, I prefer slower industrial music. If there's a crowd I prefer faster and harder in order to get the crowd worked up. I rarely have to choose my own music anymore. I just let him do his job.

As the music fills my head, I forget about the guys coming in the door, forget about the quiet club, forget about my empty purse. I just dance. The job is secondary, the money a perk. It's just me now, me and The Cure.

The group coming in the door make their way in and stand for a moment just inside, letting their eyes adjust. They confer among themselves and I know that they are making a decision about where to sit. I watch them peripherally as I spin lazily down the pole. Their decision is crucial.

If men make their way straight to the stage, it usually means that they are ready to tip, comfortable in the environment, and ready to party. If they go to the bar first, it may be because what's on stage isn't to their liking. If they sit at a table, it typically means that they're more interested in looking and aren't here to pay.

These guys head straight for the stage. There are actually nine of them, I see.

I stretch out on my back in front of them like a buffet, hips tilted, arms above my head, stomach concave, the shorts I wear stretched across my hipbones, a delightful cave of shadow forming under the fabric.

"Damn," one of the guys says to the man next to him. Money starts appearing in their hands.

I let the waitress take all their drink orders, moving slowly from one man to the next, giving each attention in turn. The stage becomes littered with dollar bills and my G-string fills up with money. The men lay a pile in front of one man, and the one in front of me leans in to whisper in my ear.

"It's all about my buddy here," he tells me.

So I go to my knees in front of the man with the pile of money, reaching for his shoulders, my cheek against his, purring into his ear, giving him a view straight between the swell of my breasts and down my stomach to the small triangle of fabric between my legs.

"Why are you so special?" I ask him.

"I just got back from a tour in Iraq," he says.

"Welcome home!" I exclaim, sitting back so that the whole row can hear me. "Happy Independence Day!" I clap, laughing.

More money appears.

They applaud enthusiastically at the end of my set and I shake their hands one by one. Back in the dressing room I count my take: $28. After brushing the shine off my nose with translucent powder, I head back out into the club. I am relieved to see that the group is still at the stage, treating the next dancer as kindly as they treated me. They have money to spend and do not appear in any hurry to go anywhere.

One of them stands at the bar and I slide in next to him. "I'm Star," I say.

"Kurt." He shakes my hand. "Do a shot with us!"

"What are you drinking?"

"Tequila."

"Hook me up."

I help him carry the drinks back to the stage where they are passed out. I obligingly lick each of their hands between thumb and forefinger, sprinkling the salt one by one.

"To our hometown heroes!" one cries exuberantly.

"To being home!" the newly returned one cries, just as enthusiastically.

We drink: salt, shot, lime slice. I feel the warmth down my throat and into my belly.

"This is Star," Kurt tells the group.

"Sit with us!" they cry.

I tilt my chin down flirtatiously. "Only if y'all tip for me." Kitten is on stage and I see her nod at me imperceptibly.

It's considered bad form for one dancer to sit at another's stage as it draws the customers' attention and negatively impacts tips. But getting the men to tip is a good ploy to make more money. I sit and immediately nine dollar bills appear on the stage in front of me.

Kitten goes to her knees and slides her arms around my neck, and I lean forward into her soft skin, smelling the floral body spray she prefers. Her lips are so close to mine that the aroma of her candy lip gloss overpowers the body spray.

The men hoot and cheer.

I hear her breath, the soft sound of her knees against the padded rail that runs round the stage. She leans away from me, head hanging toward her heels, into a backbend. The fuchsia fabric between her legs glows against her tan skin in the black light. She is beautiful.

Later, after giving two of the men private dances, I stand at the bar doing another round of shots. The money has continued to flow, maybe a bit more for me and Kitten but all the girls on the shift have been making money off the group. A few other patrons have drifted in, along with a couple of regulars, and the club is still mostly empty. But we no longer care.

"You really like that metal music, don't you?"

"What?" My attention has drifted. Now I realize that the man next to me has been talking, and I tilt my chin toward him, biting my lip, and looking up through my lashes to make up for the lapse. "What's up?"

"You ever dance to country music?"

I think about how to navigate this question. It should be pretty obvious by now that I'm not a country sort of girl, but strippers never say "no" outright.

"I really like Johnny Cash," I reply.

This is not a lie. Though I do not regularly listen to country and western, I do like the man in black, along with Willie Nelson and even some Hank, Jr.

"You know that song 'Proud to Be an American'?"

"I do," I cautiously reply.

His eyes light up. "Our buddy, you know, the one that just came home? He recorded his own version of that song."

"Really?" I feign enthusiasm, feeling a pit in my stomach. I know where this is going. "That's so awesome!"

"Can you dance to it?" His eyes are eager, excited. "That would *so* make my buddy's day."

"Sure!" I don't even hesitate, though I have no idea as to the sound quality of this recording. Or if the war hero can carry a tune. All my face shows is happiness, no hint of my reticence about dancing to a vapid song unquestioningly glorifying American patriotism. Society teaches us to view all soldiers as "heroes," no matter their actual actions. To display even a hint of criticism for the military industrial complex that receives so many tax dollars has no place in the fantasy environment of the club. This returned soldier can be convinced of the worth of his service by watching a woman take her clothes off for him while he sings about how awesome his country is. Is that the epitome of American freedom?

Happily, the quality of the CD is good and the guy can sing. The DJ pairs the song with "Born in the USA" and the nine men sing along lustily, their arms linked. I see no hint of awareness that Springsteen's song is meant to be ironic, a criticism of the draft. They let go of one another just long enough to put money on the stage, not dollar bills this time but fives and tens and twenties. I make a hundred dollars in less than ten minutes. When I count out at the end of the evening, I have broken three bills. The other girls do almost as well. Working holidays is a gamble.

Chapter Nine

In Love

Daniel is in his fifties with thinning red hair. We have virtually nothing in common; he has a high school education and is into sports and that's about it. I'm finishing my master's degree and find sports to be a boorish manifestation of hypermasculinity.

But my job is to be the perfect woman for every man. So I know how to ask intelligent enough questions to keep him talking about himself. Daniel loves to talk about himself.

"So then what happened?" I ask, leaning toward him, my gaze raptly on his face. I make a game of looking at the bridge of his nose so it looks like I'm meeting his eyes.

He's telling me a long, rambling story that started with a tailgating party and appears to be culminating with having drinks with some ball team.

"Then…then…" He's laughing so hard his eyes water. "Then Hank says, 'That's what *she said!*'" He collapses into chuckles.

I throw back my head and laugh with him, though I've lost the thread of the story and never cared in the first place. Daniel's not a bad guy but it's almost like he's not a person at all. He takes up space, talks words, and pays. He pays.

"I think it's time for you to have a private dance," I say and pull him up. He comes willingly.

I like dancing for him because then I don't have to talk to him. He pays me to sit with him as well but only to the tune of $5 a song. A private dance is $20 a song. Usually I can dance for two or three songs before he lays money on the stage, indicating that he's done.

It's hard to keep things fresh in the private dance area. The stage is a little raised platform that's about 4 feet square. The customers sit in plush chairs on the stage. The setup doesn't leave us a lot of room to move around. I compensate for my energetic floor show by moving very slowly here, making every move languid, keeping lots of eye contact, letting the customer really look. I can make one pose last half a song.

Daniel has two or three dancers he likes, so we rotate around him through the evening. When I finish my dance I catch Valentine's eye. She's sitting with one of her other customers and gives me a tiny nod in acknowledgment. She's up and now I can go hang out with one of my other regulars who has just arrived. At least he's a decent conversationalist.

In the coming weeks Daniel starts to distance himself from me. It begins when he starts only buying a single dance. Then he slacks off tipping me to sit with him. When I do sit with him, he seems distracted. It's not hard to figure out that he's watching Valentine. He's hyperaware of her every move, following her with his eyes, getting up to sit at her stage even if he's sitting with someone else. Obsession is building. I've seen it before.

"Have you noticed that Daniel isn't paying as much attention to us?" I ask Tyler. She's the other girl who has received his attention in the past.

"Oh, yeah," she says. "He's got it bad for Valentine. That cash cow has dried up."

Valentine is sitting farther down the dressing table doing her hair. "He does have a bit of a crush," she admits.

"Work it, girl," I tell her. "Dude's loaded." Daniel has some sort of middle management position and his hobbies are sports and strippers. Most of his money comes to us.

She gives herself a smile in the mirror. "He's gonna pay my bills tonight."

"Good for you," Tyler says. "Honestly, you can have him."

"He just likes me because I can talk football," Valentine says.

"Have at it." I grab my purse. "He is all yours." I head onto the floor and pass him without a glance. Peter is waiting for me, and he's worth more and can also keep up his end of a conversation. It was nice when I had the income from both regulars, but I've still got several guys on the hook. Not having to sit with Daniel will open up new possibilities.

I'm aware that Valentine sits with Daniel pretty much all night. She gives him several private dances and lavishes attention on him when she's on stage.

She'd better be careful, I think to myself. Excluding other money to milk one guy has its dangers. If that one regular loses interest, then a dancer can be left without regulars. Just dancing on stage is a lot less lucrative.

"How'd you do?" I ask at the end of the night.

"Paid my bills," Valentine replies with a smirk. "Tomorrow I'll start on next month's."

I laugh. "Good for you."

And that's what she does. Daniel arrives about 30 minutes after she does, every single night she works. All night she sits with only him. Often he is the only one sitting at her stage. Valentine has a sleek little body but nothing spectacular. She's plain in the face with hair that frizzes in the humidity. She's cute but nothing more. It takes connection to get people to the stage, or an awesome stage show, or bombshell looks. She's capable of making good connections, but now she's ignoring everyone.

I understand her choice. He's easy money and a lot of it. And it's none of my business so I pretty much forget about the whole thing.

Then Valentine announces to the dressing room one evening that she's pregnant.

This is several months later and I glance up, only half interested. I'm not close with her and don't know her that well.

Other girls rush to congratulate her with hugs and exclamations.

"How long do you plan to keep working?" Celeste asks.

"Oh, until I'm showing. I'm going to try to push it to my fifth month," Valentine answers.

"What did Seth say?" Celeste says. She has an arm around Valentine and is absently rubbing her flat belly.

"He's so excited!" Valentine exclaims. "We only just started trying."

I surmise from all this that Seth must be baby-daddy-boyfriend, and that the pregnancy is both wanted and planned.

"And look!" Valentine shows her left hand where a glittering diamond adorns her ring finger.

The chorus of congratulations begins all over again.

"We're saving up for a house," Valentine explains. "I want to be all moved in before my third trimester. Then we'll get married next year. Once I have my figure back!" She laughs.

Later that evening, passing her all snuggled up in Daniel's lap, I smirk to myself. That's what the down payment on a home looks like: middle-aged and balding.

Valentine makes good on working to the end of her fourth month. She starts to show a little, round belly but she's well aerobicized and carries the weight well.

But Daniel notices.

I find myself next to him at the bar one evening. I'm wasting time until I have to be up on stage and he's ordering a beer.

"How are you?" I ask casually.

He smiles at me. "I'm good, Star. How you been?"

"Good."

He leans closer toward me and I tilt my head toward him. "Have you noticed..." He hesitates.

"Have I noticed what?" We're whispering now, as much as one can whisper over the music.

"Valentine has gained a little weight."

I glance down at his little pudge before I can help it.

"I know," he says, catching my eye. "She just usually takes

such good care of herself."

I look him straight in the face. "I hadn't noticed," I say.

Valentine makes her last day a Saturday. We all know that she's leaving and many of the dancers pile small gifts at her place along the dressing room counter. But she carefully doesn't make a big deal about it. She sits most of the night cozied up next to Daniel. At the end of the night it's hugs all around and then she's gone, off into her new life.

I don't think about it, or her, one way or another. Dancers come and go. My focus is school and my own social life. I work but the rest of my life is quite separate.

The next Friday Daniel arrives as he has done for almost a year. I don't think about that either. My regulars are in and I'm hanging out with them, business as usual.

Then Tyler comes over and grabs me. "Can I talk to you for a minute?"

"Sure. Excuse me," I say to Peter.

"Hey, Tyler," he says and she shoots him a tight smile. Clearly there's something on her mind. Pulling a girl away from a regular is not standard operating procedure.

"What's up?" I inquire once she has me sequestered off in a corner.

"Daniel is crying," she tells me.

I gape at her. "What?"

"He just asked me where Valentine is. I said she'd quit."

I blink stupidly at her.

"I didn't know she hadn't told him!" Tyler exclaims, taking my silence as some sort of condemnation.

I hold up my hand to stop her. "Wait. You're telling me that Daniel just now found out she quit. Just now. When you told him."

Tyler is nodding. "And now he's crying! Star, I don't know what to do!"

"Oh, for fuck's sake," I curse to myself. "That was a shitty move, not to tell him." I grab Tyler by the arm. "Come on. I'll come with you to talk to him." I shoot Peter an apologetic glance and he tips me a wink.

Daniel is sitting at one of the corner tables and Tyler's right: he's openly sobbing. I pull up a chair and sit. Tyler takes the chair next to me.

I don't say anything at first, just hand Daniel a cocktail napkin. He swabs at his eyes and sniffs miserably. I pat him gently on the shoulder as he pulls himself together.

"Is she really gone?" he asks me when he's capable of speech.

"Yes," I tell him. "She retired. I can't believe she didn't tell you."

He grasps my hand desperately. "Do you have her phone number, Star?"

"I don't," I answer honestly. "I actually don't know her that well."

"But..." He hiccups. "She owes me money!"

Tyler and I glance at one another. "What do you mean?" I ask.

"I lent her a bunch of money," he explains. "Thousands of dollars."

Tyler's eyes go wide and she looks at me helplessly.

"Okay, wait," I say to buy myself time to process what he's saying. "Do you think that the money you gave her was a loan?"

"She asked me a couple weeks ago if she could borrow some money. Of course I said yes!"

This is worse than I'd thought. He's still holding my hand and I give his fingers a squeeze and then draw away.

"Okay, Daniel. This is going to be hard for you to hear, but it's really important and you need to listen."

His wet eyes are on mine, still streaming, but at least the sobs have stopped.

I give it to him straight. "No money that changes hands in a club like this is ever a loan." I wait for my words to sink in.

"You mean...?"

"You gave her that money and you're not getting it back. She took it and she's gone."

The tears stop as though a faucet has been turned off. "I can't believe..." His words trail off.

I gesture around. "Nothing here is real, Daniel. Valentine was not your friend. She was a woman you paid to see naked. That's it. It wasn't nice of her to let you think that you were loaning her money, but it happened. All you can do is get over it."

"I can go to the police." His tears are rapidly being replaced with anger.

"No, you can't," I explain. "You gave a stripper cash money in a strip club. There's no written contract. Do you even know her real name?"

"Her name is Valentine," he says confusedly. "She's Russian, named after her grandmother."

"Her name is not Valentine, I can tell you that with absolute certainty."

"Is your name Star?" he asks.

"Of course not," I snap. I can't believe that he's this naive.

He glances at Tyler.

"Nope," she says.

"But...what's your name?" he asks me. "If it's not Star?"

"That's none of your business. We work under pseudonyms so that men like you don't stalk us after work." If I'm going to be straight with him I may as well explain the whole deal. He has clearly missed learning the rules of strip clubs.

"I need to find her," he says.

"No," I say. "If you look for her she can have you arrested for stalking and slap a restraining order on you. What you need to do, what you will do, is walk out of here right now and never come back. You just learned a very expensive lesson. Take it for what it's worth and leave."

He glares at me. "I can't believe this."

"Believe it." I rise and pull Tyler up with me. "Goodbye, Daniel." I turn and walk away without a backward glance. As I pass Rodney, one of the bouncers, I tip my head toward the corner where Daniel sits. Rodney pushes himself off the wall he's leaned against and heads over.

Chapter Ten

Skin

Ebony has skin the color of jet. She is one of the darkest people I have ever seen and she is breathtaking. The only way I can describe her is that her skin *glows* dark. Strikingly, her eyes are a light brown, golden in the lights flashing on stage. She is full-figured and voluptuous, her body moving in serpentine ripples. In DayGlo colors that catch the black lights, she is unbelievable.

I watch her from the corner of my eye as I sit at the dressing table and put the finishing touches on my hair. The palate of her makeup is the opposite of mine and I am fascinated. To contour cheekbones I use a darker color. She uses a lighter color. The blush crème she rubs into her cheeks is the color of wine. She uses a bright gold bronzer along the tops of her cheeks and sparkly gold eye shadow.

At work, Ebony wears a wig of waist-length black. Her natural hair is kinky, standing out in a short halo of tight curls. She covers this with a wig cap and affixes the fake hair, carefully fanning the bangs across her forehead. She's beautiful both ways and I cannot stop looking at her velvety skin. She is terrifyingly perfect and I'm afraid to speak to her.

Upon first meeting her I smiled and said, "Ebony? Well, that's descriptive."

Her eyes flashed at me. "Well, it's not like I'm gonna fool anyone into thinking I'm white."

"Um…" I stuttered. "No, I imagine not." *Why would she want to be white?* I wondered. *I would kill for that skin.* I wanted to place my hand against her just to admire the contrast.

She grinned dismissively and, to my knowledge, never looked at me again.

It takes me a while to realize that Ebony makes significantly less money than I do. I first become aware of this while eavesdropping on her conversation with another dancer. The two of them compare their nightly take, and Ebony names a dollar amount $60 less than the other (white) girl. I do not initially think anything of it—our nightly earnings vary depending on the clientele and whether or not we had regulars.

But then I overhear her again several weeks later. "You white girls make all the cash," she tells another girl.

Can that be true? I wonder incredulously. So I start paying attention.

Over the years I worked with a number of black girls and Latina. The black girls make about half of what the white girls make. They have fewer regulars, and those that they do have do not spend as much. The Latina girls make about two-thirds of what the white girls make. Some of them sell themselves as having a more exotic pedigree: Asian, Spanish, even Moorish. They exoticize themselves for American consumption.

It's more difficult to get hired as a woman of color. I never saw a white girl get turned down for a stripper position. But I saw black girls get refused for auditions entirely. I once heard a manager say, "Sorry. We already have black girls on both shifts."

That semester in college I took Feminist Philosophy. I considered myself a feminist because I believe in equal rights, but the concept of intersectionality had never really occupied my thoughts.

The class, like most classes on women's studies or gender, consisted of 14 women and no men. I was surprised by this because the class was taught by a popular professor in the philosophy department. In classes I had taken with her previously, the scale usually tipped slightly in favor of male students. I did not yet realize that men don't think gender is about them.

In terms of race, the class was ten white women and four black women. We read Judith Butler and Alison Jaggar and discussed the role of emotion and gender in epistemology. I understood the material, but I began to have a nagging feeling that maybe, by focusing on sexism, we are actually perpetuating it. I think of feminism as a lens and, like any lens, it can teach us to see abuse where there actually isn't any. I began to wonder if the women in the class were seeing sexism where none existed.

One day several weeks into the semester, I finally voiced my concern. "I've never been discriminated against for being female," I said. "I don't think anyone has ever taken me less seriously because I'm a girl."

The black woman sitting next to me rolled her eyes. "Yeah, but look at you," she said.

"What do you mean?"

She leaned in closer to me, and to this day I give her credit for not just laughing in my naive face. "You're white," she explained patiently. "You look like a Barbie doll. Of course people take you seriously. Or at least act like they do. They're probably trying to look down your shirt."

That moment was the first time that the concept of privilege, and the recognition that I have some, clicked for me. I began to understand intersectionality: the concept that every person is an intersection of privileges and oppressions, and that different social constructs like race and gender identity intersect and influence one another. The fact that I am white decreases (though does not eliminate) the sexism I experience in my life. Women of color are more likely to experience sexism in addition to racism.

This brings me to Elizabeth.

I meet Elizabeth in a high-end club in a small, wealthy town in a western state several years later. She comes bouncing into the club one afternoon and asks to audition. In stocking feet she might stand 5 feet 2 inches and she is a big girl: wide thighs, swelling ass, baby-fat tummy, breasts that spill over her tank top. She has a round face and round blue eyes all framed in a shoulder-length mop of frizzy curly hair of a nondescript ash color. She has a wide smile that makes me and the day-shift manager spontaneously smile back. She also has an unmistakable Irish accent.

Aaron is both tending bar and managing the club. He glances at me and lifts his eyebrows. "Sure!" I say. "I'll take you back to the dressing room so you can change."

I take her backstage and show her where she can leave her clothes. "Have you danced before?" I inquire.

"No, but I'm here on a student visa and I can't work a real job. And I've always wanted to try it!" Elizabeth strips off her clothes with no hint of modesty and pulls on department store lingerie: lacy bra with matching thong panties, garter belt with stockings, and a sheer nightie that ties across her breasts and just covers her bottom. She straps on sandals with a blocky 3-inch heel.

Baby heels, I think with a smirk. I wear a custom outfit of crisscrossing black straps and interconnected rings. A black bikini top with silver studs covers my breasts, and the whole ensemble is topped with a floor-length sheer jacket through which my bare skin glows. In addition, I wear a metal collar with inch-long spikes, and four of my fingers are encased in jointed silver rings that cover the entire finger. Thigh-high patent leather boots with a 5-inch heel complete the look. I wear almost a thousand dollars' worth of clothing and accessories. I look like I just walked off a movie set.

Elizabeth is unfazed by me. I am not used to being taken in stride. Everything about my presentation is designed to provoke awe. But she is so friendly and bubbly that I find myself sharing that I go to the same college, that I went to Oxford for a bit during undergrad, and that I have never been to Ireland. When she's ready I briefly explain stage protocol.

"You'll audition on stage one and you can pick your own music. Wait until the second song to take your top off. Don't touch the customers once your top is off. And make sure to keep your crotch covered. Not even a pubic hair can show."

She nods seriously, never taking those blue eyes off me. I take her to the DJ booth and turn her over to the day-shift music guy.

A few minutes later she takes the stage. There are three customers sitting at the railing. One gets up and leaves but the other two look at her with interest.

She can't dance at all but she wriggles and gyrates enthusiastically. A lot of new girls have little body control and less rhythm. Some women never truly learn grace and the fluid movements of stripping. I peg her as one of those.

She has no fear of the men sitting at stage and kneels in front of them, bumping and grinding with gusto. She says something and they lean toward her, rapt, and she beams her thousand-volt smile.

Aaron elects to hire her and I work with Elizabeth for nine months, the length of her course in the United States before she returns to Ireland. Unlike Ebony, Elizabeth rakes in the cash. She makes more money than most of the girls in the club, myself included. Her personality shines from her like a beacon, and her hearty laugh and thrilling accent light up the entire club. In appearance she is homely according to social conventions, mousy even. But her confidence level is like nothing I have ever encountered. She loves the club, adores dancing, dotes on people, and appears to have not a single iota of concern for her appearance. Confidence truly is the most beautiful thing.

Surrounded by women with fake tits, women who starved and bleached, plucked and concealed, Elizabeth radiated honesty and self-esteem. She and Ebony are like bookends in my memory, juxtaposed examples of the complexity of femininity and race in the modern world. Ebony remains one of the most sensual people I have ever seen. Hers was a blistering, overwhelming beauty. Elizabeth was her complete opposite: plain and plump. But she, too, had an overwhelming personality. Ebony taught me that race matters. Elizabeth taught me that looks are not everything. As long as you're white.

Chapter Eleven

Creep Show

Walking through the door my identity shifts, as it does every night. My walk turns to a seductive saunter, my lips curl up, my chin lowers as my daylight persona transforms into the person I become at night. This transformation has become routine; I hardly notice it anymore. Both aspects are deeply *me*, rooted in different parts of my personality. Some dancers feel like they must adopt a mask in the club. I never feel that way: I just tap into another part of myself.

I nod a casual greeting to the doorman, handing him my bag of clothing and makeup case to carry.

"How you doin'?" he asks, stepping back to allow me to pass.

"Ask me in an hour," I reply, leading the way across the floor of the club toward the dressing room, which is up three steps and through a double layer of black curtain. Sometimes the bouncers hide in the foot of space between the curtains, grabbing us as we come by, delighting in their ability to make us squeal.

I scan the club quickly, looking for familiar faces. It is still too early for things to really be hopping, but one of my regulars likes to show up early, timing his arrival to mine so that he has me all to himself for a couple of hours before I get busy.

A day-shift girl spins lazily down the pole on stage one, reaching to grab the shirtfront of the lone customer, pulling his face into her breasts. The club is quiet and the only men I recognize are the day-shift barflies, clustered around the bar, one eye on the stage, the rest of their attention on the tall tale spun by Holiday, a biker who has been coming to play pool and drink $5 beers for most of the 20 years the club has been open.

"I swear that cop was 7 feet tall if he was an inch," Holiday swore and a line of heads nodded in contemplative agreement, not believing a word but engrossed in the story nonetheless.

"Anyone looks 7 feet tall to a shortie like you," I call across the bar, and the row of heads turns toward me: seven pairs of eyes traveling as one down the length of my body. I toss my hair and they all laugh on cue.

"I may be short," Holiday retorts, taking a swig of beer. "But I got it where it counts, baby."

I laugh back at them. "I bet you do." Turning, I let them watch me walk across the floor, the doorman trailing with my belongings.

I claim my spot on the long counter that serves as our dressing table and spin the lock on my combination, opening a locker stuffed with clothing. I quickly pull out micro shorts and matching top. I select a G-string, red to complement the black velvet outfit, from the hoop of underwear hung from a hook in my locker, and lacy socks, black with red bows. Last, I remove my shoes from the pile at the bottom. They are black patent pumps with 5-inch heels and an ankle strap.

I shuck my day clothes, jeans and a tank top, and complete the transformation. I typically do my hair and makeup at home to give myself a few more minutes of solitude, arriving ten minutes or so before shift change. I fold my normal clothes and place them neatly at the front of my locker. My boots and coat go on a rack between the rows of lockers.

I powder my nose quickly and apply lipstick. Removing vanilla body spray from my makeup case, I spritz it over my hair and under my arms. Last is jewelry: spiked dog collar, wooden hoops that look like gauges but aren't, an arm band in the shape of a dragon, and the rings for which I've become famous. On the thumb of my right hand is a thick silver band with a single hooked talon. On my ring finger slides a jointed sheath that slips over my wedding ring, hiding it. There's a matching one for the middle finger of the right hand. And then the most spectacular ring on the forefinger of my left hand: it covers my entire finger from the top joint, hooking out past my fingertip in a claw. It is jointed twice for my knuckles. I like to tap that metal hook on the stage; it's a great attention getter.

I look quickly in the mirror, doing a last check for stray hairs, uncovered blemishes, smears. But I am perfect, a cyborg vampire in velvet and leather.

I hear the call for shift change, and all of us in the dressing room head out to the stages. The day-shift girls take our places in the dressing room.

I pick the least crowded stage and drop slowly into the splits, stretching languorously, warming up my muscles. Kris waltzes onto stage and drops behind me, stretching herself out in a mirror image.

"How are you?" I ask her over my shoulder. "How was the party last night?"

She laughs her husky chuckle. "Well, I didn't get laid but I got in a fight."

I crane my head back to look at her. She's probably the most naturally beautiful woman I have ever seen, with perfect white skin, almond-shaped hazel eyes, and deep black hair curling to her waist. She's also intimidatingly heterosexual so I admire her from afar. "Are you being serious?" I inquire.

"Yep."

"A fight?" She is so reserved that I find this hard to imagine. "Did you win?"

She grins smugly. "I did."

"Who did you fight?"

"Some girl I went to high school with. We didn't get along then and she started talking smack about me, telling everyone I'm a stripper whore."

I can't imagine anyone less whorish than Kris. "So what did you do?"

"I punched her in the nose." She holds up bruised knuckles as proof.

"What'd *she* do?" I ask.

Kris shoots me her sardonic grin again. "Cried."

I laugh out loud, amused by the image of decorous Kris punching someone in the face. It's so incongruous. "Well, sorry about the not getting laid part."

She sits up on her knees and arcs into a slow backbend, stretching her arms out to each side. "I've never been in a fight. It was kind of interesting."

"I've never been in a fight either," I reply, waggling my fingers at the DJ who stands in the middle of the club writing down our names. He'll form the set lists that will dictate the order we dance. I hope I'm paired with Kris. The girl on stage one always dictates the music and the two of us like the same stuff, heavy, dark, and melodic. I can dance to pretty much anything but I have my preferences, and my regulars like it when I strip to things that obviously turn me on. The music is a crapshoot, though. Kris and I are similar enough in style to steal customers from one another. It can be better to be up with girls who are entirely different.

One time an owner tried to tell me that I couldn't dance to metal anymore because it turned the customers off. I responded by laying three 100-dollar bills on the bar and asking if he wanted me to keep tipping out 10%. I argued that diversity is actually a good thing for a club because it brings in a diverse customer base. He relented.

The song ends and I swing by the DJ booth to see when I'm up. Three sets, that's six songs, or about 30 minutes. I scan the club but none of my regulars have shown yet. I'm a bit of an introvert and pick the people I talk to carefully. A lot of strippers make the majority of their money by hustling private dances, but I've never been able to just walk up and ask a guy if he wants to drop 20 bucks on a private dance. I make the majority of my money from regular customers with whom I've established relationships.

I spot a familiar face. He's been in before and tipped well on stage, but I haven't had the chance to meet him. I stroll over to the table where he sits alone a couple of rows back from stage one. "May I sit with you?"

A smile lights up his face. "Of course. Yes! Please." He leaps up and pulls the chair out for me.

I sit and hold out my hand. "I'm Natasha. I don't believe we've formally met."

"Keith. I'm very pleased that you came over."

Waitresses are programmed to approach a table anytime a dancer sits down with a customer. We generate a huge profit for the club by getting customers to buy us drinks. Lela walks up and asks if we would like anything.

Keith tips his beer bottle, which is mostly full. "I'm fine for now."

Lela looks pointedly at me.

"Oh!" Keith stutters. "Of course. Would you like anything?"

I smile at him. "Thank you, I'll have a seven-and-seven."

Lela heads off toward the bar. "Thank you," I tell Keith again.

"My pleasure," he says.

He's young, probably around 30, with a boyishly pleasing face. He wears a white shirt with narrow blue pinstripes, jeans, and loafers. He looks like he got off work from somewhere that has cubicles.

"So, Keith." I lean toward him slightly, resting my elbows on the table. The pose pushes my breasts up provocatively. If he looks it's peripherally. "You know what I do for a living. What do you do?"

"I work as an accountant for a brewery." He names one of the local microbreweries.

I almost smile. Of course he's an accountant. "Well, I'm glad there are people in the world who are accountants so that the rest of us don't have to be."

He laughs. "You have to do stuff besides this." His gesture

encompasses the stages, the bar, the shadowed corners where men lean toward glittering women with shining exposed skin. "Who else are you?"

"I'm a college student," I say.

"What do you study?"

"Religion."

He gapes at me. My answer usually takes people off guard. "And you work here?"

"Why not?" I ask. "The money is good and I have plenty of time to study."

"But..." He searches for words. "How can you be religious and work here?"

I laugh. "I didn't say that I'm religious. I said that I study religion. Not to mention the fact that sexuality and religion don't have to be contradictions."

Now he's intrigued. "My Catholic upbringing taught me that sex is the vehicle of original sin."

"Well, that's one interpretation. Christianity in all its forms often conflates sex with sin. And I think that's a shame. Sex doesn't have to be shameful. Plus," I gesture at Kris on stage one. "She's not having sex with anyone." I glance pointedly around the club. "No one here is having sex. We're just being sexy." I grin at him.

He smiles back. "You are sexy."

I stretch one tan leg out and run my hand down it. "Yes, I am."

He snorts. "And modest."

Now I laugh out loud. "Not a bit."

"So...I take it that you're not Christian?"

I glance at him from beneath my lashes. "Is that a problem?"

"No. It just makes you more intriguing."

"You're easy to impress."

He takes a swallow of beer. "I don't think so. You caught my eye because you really know how to dance."

"Thank you." I sip from the drink Lela sets before me. "I like to dance. Always have."

"Have you thought about working someplace like Vegas?" He hands Lela a bill and waves her away, signaling that he doesn't need change.

"I have. But I'm really just doing this to put myself through school. I don't think I have what it takes to be a career stripper."

"What does it take to be a career stripper?"

"Well, girls who really want to make money work a seasonal circuit. It includes Vegas but also the east coast and places like Alaska. They hit all the rallies like Sturgis in North Dakota. Bike week. The car shows and races."

"So you'd have to travel a lot."

"Yes. I have thought about it. But I need to finish school first."

"That makes sense."

I shift the conversation back to him. "How long have you been coming here? I've seen you a few times."

"Just a few months. It gets me out of the house."

"Is that a problem for you?" I make my voice light, teasing. "Getting out of the house?"

He looks down. "I'm going through some things right now."

I sober immediately. "I'm sorry to hear that. We can certainly offer distraction here!"

He smiles but isn't quite ready to meet my eyes. I wonder if it's divorce, a breakup, or something else. There is an earnest, sad quality to him.

"My cousin and I grew up really close," he tells me. "Like brothers. We're the same age, just a week apart. We live together." He hesitates. "Lived together."

I think very quickly. He's about to divulge something to me and I have to figure out, in the space of about two seconds, if I should let him. If I choose incorrectly, I will embarrass and isolate him. I make my decision based on the slight quiver in his voice and his vulnerability. I decide that what he really needs is someone to listen.

I lean across the table and place my hand on his arm, just above his wrist. His shirtsleeve is pulled down and so I make contact without actually touching his skin. It's reassuring without being too intimate. "What happened?" I ask.

He looks up at me and I meet his gaze unflinchingly. His eyes gleam a little but his voice is steady. "He passed away recently."

I do not look away or change expression. "I'm so sorry." I apply a slight, gentle pressure to his arm. "How did it happen?"

He looks down. "Cancer."

"Ugh." I make a disgusted noise. "That bitch."

There are definitely tears in his eyes now but he smiles a bit at my words. "Yes, that nasty bitch."

"Was it fast at least?"

"Yes. Relatively."

"What kind of cancer?"

"Lung cancer." He swipes his eyes and makes a sound of grim humor. "Never smoked a day in his life."

I sigh audibly. "That really and truly sucks. I'm so sorry, Keith. I get why you need to get out of the house."

I hear my name called as the next dancer to stage. It's bad timing; I need to sit with him for a few more minutes to make sure that he isn't about to get uncomfortable with opening up to me. I lean close to him, so he can feel my breath in his ear and against his neck. "I know what loss is like."

He glances up at me very quickly and then away again. "You do?"

"I do." I hold close to him for a second longer and then sit back. "I have to go to stage. But I'd like to continue this conversation when I'm done. Is that okay?"

His eyes are dry again when he smiles at me. He has no difficulty meeting my gaze. "I'd like that a lot."

I get up and walk to stage one, setting my purse and drink on the top step. It's in the sight line of the DJ, who makes sure that nothing gets stolen and no one spikes our drinks.

I wait until the girl on stage collects the bills littering the stage and then take her place. I climb the pole at the corner of the stage and spin lazily down as the opening strains of my first song sound through the speakers. There are several men at the stage and the dollars start to appear. For the moment I ignore them and slither off the pole onto my back, flipping into a somersault that leaves me on my hands and knees. I straighten up, staying on my knees, and move into a backbend, feeling my belly narrow and tighten, my hips jutting forward. I let my head touch the stage and slide all the way down, knees bent tight on either side. This is why I don't like platform shoes: gripping with my toes, I slide up the stage and straighten my legs, ending up lying flat on my back. I lift both legs straight overhead, clapping my shoes together sharply and then opening my legs all the way, banging my heels on the stage on either side. Sitting up I am in full splits. It's a neat, flexible, sensuous show and the audience claps. I see Keith has come to stage.

I work my way around, performing for each man for a minute before collecting their dollars. I push each bill down in my G-string to create a little fan of money on each hip. When I get to Keith I kneel before him and put my arms around his shoulders, leaning in, covering him with my hair. It's more intimate than I've been with the other customers, but he has a five in front of him and I'm happy to see him at stage. It means that he's not embarrassed that he opened up to me. He has promise.

Keith comes in to see me every couple of weeks. He's not a big spender but he's worth a bill each visit. And I like him. He's painfully shy and I learn that he's never really had a girlfriend. I wonder if he's a virgin.

"I can't talk to women," he confides in me.

"You're talking to me," I point out.

"But I'm paying you."

I narrow my eyes at him. "Well, that is true. But I'm not the sort of person to talk to someone I don't like." I grin. "Even if they pay me."

He looks at me like he doesn't really believe me.

"Would I lie to you?" I ask, lifting an eyebrow.

He smiles his shy smile. "I don't think so."

I know him well enough now to take his hand. I'm close enough to slide my knee between his. He always blushes when I get so close to him. I blow on his red cheeks, teasingly. "Cool you off."

"I don't think that's possible." He turns redder.

I stand up abruptly, pulling him up with me. "Time for your private dance."

He flushes even more alarmingly but allows me to lead him into the private area. I plant him in a reclining chair and climb into his lap. He keeps his hands obediently at his sides.

Putting a knee on either arm of the chair and my hands on his shoulders I purr into his ear. "You shouldn't be afraid of women." My breasts push into his chest. "You're nice, you're cute, you have a good job."

His eyes slip closed. The flush drains from his cheeks and his breath comes faster.

I take one leg and then the other off the arms of the chair and brace my toes against the floor. Holding my weight steady with my arms I slide down. I never actually touch any part of him between his chest and his knees but I'm close enough to feel the heat from his body on my skin. It's all about the tease, the artifice, the fantasy. It's about seeming to do so much more than I actually am.

"I'm cute?" he asks, his eyes still closed.

I laugh throatily. "Yes. You're cute."

He opens his eyes and I see it: he's in love with me. Or thinks he is. He's in love with the idea of me, the projection of me.

"Maybe I should be giving you the private dance," he says.

I grip his knees and stand up, spinning so that my back is to him. I hook my thumbs through the waistband of the skintight red velvet pants I'm wearing and bend forward oh, so slowly, revealing the matching G-string underneath.

Keith sighs.

"But I am much better at teasing than you are," I tell him.

"Yes," he breathes.

Six months later he tells me that he's met a woman.

"That's wonderful!" I say. I mean it. He's a sweet guy. "Who is she? What does she do? Tell me everything!"

He gazes at me pensively. I have time to wonder what he's thinking and then he says, "You're not jealous." It's a statement of fact, not a question.

I lost him, I think. "No," I reply softly. "Of course not. I'm delighted for you."

He reflects on this for a moment. Then he says, "She's a temp at the office where I work. I think she likes me."

"Why do you think she likes you?"

He looks up at me shyly. "She told me."

"That's great!" I crow. "I like her. I love it when women just say what they mean. She actually said, 'I like you'?"

"She asked me out."

I laugh, delighted. "What did you say?"

"I said that I would. But I set the date out a bit. It's in ten days."

"Why did you do that?"

"Well..." he hesitates. "Because of you."

Shit. I think quickly but he beats me to the punch.

"Don't say anything. I know how it is. This." His gesture encompasses the club. "This isn't real. And I know that. I just... wanted to be sure. And..." He rushes to continue. "And I'm nervous."

"About what?"

"The last time I went on a date was ten years ago."

"Okay, let's think about this. What do you plan to do on this date?"

"Dinner and a movie?"

I nod. "Sure, that's certainly an option. But I'd recommend something a little more memorable."

"Like what?"

"It's warm. Why not a picnic?"

He looks at me doubtfully.

I laugh. "Hear me out. It's less formal than a restaurant. You don't have to worry about etiquette or tipping the waiter. You can scope the location out ahead of time. It will give you both the entirety of the great outdoors to look at if you get nervous or the conversation stalls."

His doubt starts to shift into interest.

"Afterwards you can take a walk and that will give you a break from looking at one another. Walking lets you take a breather from conversation and you can talk about what you see."

He starts to nod.

"Just plan really well." I shake my finger under his nose. "Do your homework."

"What do you mean?"

"You need to find out if she has any food allergies and what she likes to drink. The last thing you want to do is serve beer only to find out that she doesn't drink alcohol."

He looks dismayed.

"Don't buy messy food. Plan on something that's easy to eat off a plate in your lap. Don't bring a blanket, that's too intimate. Bring two nice folding chairs." I look sternly at him. "And make sure they're clean."

"I feel like I should be taking notes!"

"You'll do fine. Check movie schedules ahead of time. I'd recommend checking to see if there are any movies in the park coming up. Give her two or three choices and then let her choose."

He grins at me. "You give good dating advice."

I pat his hand. "Let me know how it goes."

The next time I see him is when he tells me that his date went perfectly. He describes his new amore as fun and talkative. I hug him and tell him, again, how happy I am for him.

"But I don't think I'll see her again."

"What?" I'm surprised. "Why not? You seem like you really hit it off!"

He shrugs. "I can't really explain it."

I look at him sternly. "Try."

He looks away from me. "I guess I'm not really the dating type."

"So what are you? The lifelong bachelor type?"

He grins. "Maybe so, yeah."

"But you seemed like you really liked this woman. You were really excited. What happened?"

He finally looks back and meets my eyes. "I don't want to have sex with her."

I wonder again if he's a virgin. "You mean that you're not attracted to her?"

"Oh, I am. But I won't be if I have sex with her."

I'm baffled. "What on earth do you mean?"

He makes a small moue of disgust. "I can never stay attracted to a woman once I've had sex with her."

I'm so astonished that I can't think what to say. There's a much bigger pathology here than I had realized. "Is that why you come to strip clubs? Because you can pay women to be sexual and not have to fuck them?"

He shrugs. "I guess so. It's also why I only have sex with prostitutes."

Nope, not a virgin. "Oh," I manage. In the space of a few minutes my perception of him has shifted entirely. I had pegged him as a shy guy who gets tongue-tied around women. Now, I'm realizing that he can't respect women if he knows that they have sex. He needs to be able to believe that we're Madonnas even while he pays us to play the whore.

"Would you fuck me for money?"

He's never spoken to me like this before and at first I can only gape at him. "NO. Of course not!" I snarl finally.

He nods with a small smile of satisfaction. "I thought not. You're one of the good ones."

"Good what?" I'm struggling to keep up with this sudden turn of events.

"Good girls. You're one of the good girls."

I wonder what he would do if I told him that I have sex. That I enjoy sex. That sexual play with a partner I'm into is fun and pleasurable. I would become the whore. Simply for admitting that I enjoy sex would transform me from the sexually desirable but untouchable ideal into the dirty and undesirable.

He pushes back from the table. "I'm ready for my private dance."

I stand up abruptly. "In just a minute. Let me run to the dressing room for a second."

He shoots me a dark look. Suddenly, he's all orders and demands.

I place my hand on his shoulder, mollifying. "I'll be right back." I feel him relax beneath my hand.

It's all I can do not to run across the floor to get away from him. He's making my skin crawl.

In the dressing room Savannah sees the expression on my face. "What's up?" she asks.

I throw the metal purse I carry my money in onto the dressing room counter with a clatter. "One of my regulars just went total creep show on me."

"Ugh," she says. "The worst. What did he do?"

"I just found out that he only has sex with prostitutes because he can't respect women who have sex with him."

"What?" she laughs.

"That's exactly what *I* said!" I exclaim. "I mean, I think he's seriously screwed up."

She shrugs. "Aren't most of the men who come in here?"

Are they? Is she right? I lean on the counter and take a deep breath, looking into my eyes in the mirror. Lined with thick black shadow they are very blue in the bright lights.

A lot of times this job makes me feel like a therapist. I'd thought that I could help Keith and others like him, repair some of the damage this world had done to their self-esteem. I'd assumed that I could fix him and that he would start a normal relationship with a real woman and that I'd never see him again. But this is beyond my ability to fix.

I straighten up and take deep red lipstick from my makeup case. It's so dark it's almost black and I apply it carefully, turning my mouth from glossy pink to vampire.

I pick up my purse and smile ruefully at Savannah. "Time to go give creep show his private dance."

She pumps her fist at me. "Go get him, girl."

Chapter Twelve

The Virgin

"I think Todd's really cute," Kitty tells me.

I glance at her in the mirror, pausing in the delicate act of applying liquid eyeliner to my lids. Todd is a bartender and I don't know him well, but he is nicely proportioned in a jock-y kind of way. Not my type.

"Yeah?" I prompt noncommittally.

"I think I'm going to ask him out."

"He gets around," I say, not really as a warning but more as a statement of fact. Todd has probably screwed a dozen of the dancers in the time I've worked at this club. None of them seem to mind when he moves on, which makes me think that he communicates the terms of his intentions well and doesn't leave a trail of devastation in his wake. This is something I can admire about him.

"Really?" Kitty pauses brushing pale pink lip gloss onto her mouth.

"Is that a problem?" I inquire, returning to my artistry. I like to get the sweep of eyeliner just right.

"Well, I guess guys are supposed to sleep around," she says doubtfully.

"First of all, sleeping around is not a 'guy' thing." This sexual essentialism bullshit drives me crazy. "Anyone can sleep around. Or not. It's about the individuals, not about guys and girls. Secondly, I guess it's only a problem if you want something long-term. I figure, you think he's hot, he thinks you're hot, have at it." I admire the perfect cat eye I have created.

Kitty sits down in one of the straight-backed chairs along the dressing table. She's only been at the club about a month, but I've become a confidante because I let her come home with me one night when she didn't have anywhere to go. Her mom had kicked her out when the stripping came out, and her apartment wouldn't be ready until the end of the month. I let her crash in the guest room a few times. She's nice enough, but in my opinion she lacks a personality. So I kind of treat her like a pet.

Now she looks like she might cry. "I want him to be my first," she finally mumbles.

I freeze in the act of patting glitter across my eyelids and then set the brush down slowly. "What?" I ask, turning from the mirror so that I can look straight into her face. "Your *first*?"

"Yes," she murmurs, looking down at her hands.

I sit down to bring my eyes even with hers. "Are you telling me that you're a virgin?"

"Yes." She glances quickly up at me and then back down at her hands.

"How old are you?" I'm less surprised that a sexually inexperienced young woman is working as a stripper than I am at an adult virgin.

"Nineteen."

I sit for a minute just collecting my thoughts. Most immediately, Todd strikes me as a colossally bad idea. He would certainly get the job done, but this girl lacks a certain emotional maturity. She's looking for true love.

Apparently my silence is weirding her out because she asks, "How old were you?"

"Sixteen," I reply. "But that doesn't really matter. It's more about...timing. Obviously the timing hasn't been right for you. Which means that you're smart to wait."

"Really? You don't think I'm a freak?"

I laugh. "No. I don't think you're a freak. Someone who takes care with their sexuality is anything but a freak in my book."

"But you don't think it should be Todd."

"I don't know," I tell her honestly. "It depends on what you want. It can be good for the first time to be with someone experienced. Sex is awkward and a little painful the first time. It can really help if your partner knows what they're doing. Todd certainly fits the bill. But that boy is not looking to settle. He has access to a string of pussy, and he knows a good thing when he sees it."

"You think he's a bad person."

"No! That's not what I'm saying. I actually think he's a good guy. And I also know that he is not looking for a girlfriend."

"I kind of just want to do it. Get it over with."

I reach out and give her shoulders a squeeze. "Then Todd might be your guy!"

Just then the door opens and two other dancers come in, chattering about something. Kitty quickly brushes her eyes and goes back to her makeup. I take that as a cue that the conversation is over.

Later that week Kitty ends up at my house again. She had some sort of squabble with her new roommate and asks to crash with me. The next morning, over omelets, she brings it up again.

"I've decided that Todd isn't the one."

I take a bite and say nothing.

"He took Destiny home two nights ago."

I laugh. "That doesn't surprise me." Destiny is newly divorced and just settled custody. She's happy to be kid-free every other week, and I've sensed that she's looking for some good rebound sex.

"So it is painful the first time?" Kitty's cheeks flush slightly.

I set my fork down. "It depends. It can be. If you're aroused it's a lot better."

Her flush deepens.

"Look." I reach across the table and touch her hand so that she'll look at me. "If you blush every time you talk about sex, you might not be ready to have it."

She's just four years younger than me but, right now, I

feel like her mother. She just graduated high school and I just graduated with a master's degree. She's living on her own for the first time and I live in an apartment with my spouse as we look for a house to buy. She's been dancing for four months and I am about to retire after five years and move on to what will become my career. We are light years apart.

"How far have you gone before?"

"Almost all the way. Everything but, really."

"Have you had oral sex?"

Her face is positively on fire now. "Given."

"But not received."

She nods, a sheet of hair sliding forward to hide her face. "I'm worried that it...that my...you know. That it *smells*."

I laugh. I can't help it. Girls are fed a diet of ads and locker room horror stories about feminine hygiene that play on body insecurities, especially the perceived messiness of the female body, and they grow into women convinced that there's something wrong with them.

She looks at me when I laugh, her eyes narrowing defensively.

"Of course it smells!" I say and she gapes at me. "It should smell like a healthy vagina. Which, I'm sorry, does *not* smell like fish, or metal, or raw meat, or any of the hundreds of other things people think vaginas smell like. Vaginas just smell like what they are. And a woman's smell is unique to her and changes a little depending on diet, the time of the month, the pH of her body, and so on. If you're worried about a strong odor, that can be a sign that there's something wrong and you should get an exam. Otherwise, relax. If any partner ever tells you that there's something wrong with your body, dump him."

Her mouth hangs open slightly at the end of this tirade. "Thank you," she says finally. "I think I really needed to hear that."

She takes another bite of her omelet and then asks, "Should I tell the guy that I'm a virgin?"

I've picked up my fork, but now I set it down again and take a sip of coffee to collect my thoughts. "You should always communicate with your partner. You should feel comfortable discussing birth control and getting tested for STIs. You should talk about what feels good and if anything doesn't. So yes, you should tell him. But you don't have to make a big deal about it."

She nods thoughtfully.

It gets out at the club that Kitty hasn't had sex. I don't know whom else she tells, but pretty soon all the employees know and half of the regulars. She looks like the girl next door and now she's the *virgin* next door. It amazes me how her earning power rises when men find out. She becomes an object of fascination, her stage crowded with men eager to get a look at the virgin stripper. She gets outrageous propositions, offers to buy her virginity.

"Some dude just offered me $10,000!" she exclaims one evening in the dressing room.

"Get the cash up front and skip town," Liberty advises.

"Ugh, you're so nasty," Lenore says, hitting Liberty in the arm. "You should save your flower for someone special," she advises Kitty. "It should be a special present that you give to a special person."

I gag a little and roll my eyes. Lenore catches my look and glares at me.

"Don't listen to her," Barbie contradicts Lenore. "It's painful and awkward, just get it over with. Make sure the guy's decent and just do it."

"I agree," Katrina chimes in. "Once you do it then you can get on to the good stuff."

"What good stuff?" Bette inquires.

This query is met with a chorus of laughter and hoots.

"Orgasms," Katrina explains patiently. "You know, pleasure?"

Bette shrugs. "Ain't no man ever done that for me."

"Then you are doing it *wrong!*" Katrina says, backed by a

murmur of agreement.

"Maybe you should let a woman try," I suggest and laugh when Bette gapes at me.

Kitty's head swivels from person to person like she's watching a particularly engaging sporting event.

I hear my name called to stage. I pat Kitty on the shoulder. "Don't listen to this shit," I tell her. "Just do what's right for you."

"That is some hippy bullshit right there and you know it," Liberty tells me.

I give her the finger over my shoulder on the way out the door. I hear her caw laughter.

Kitty finally did have sex with a nice boy that she met at a Memorial Day parade. She told me that it didn't hurt as much as she thought it would and confessed that his fumbling attempt at oral beforehand helped a lot. She said that she bled a little and that he fetched her an ice cube wrapped in a washcloth and held her all night before taking her out for breakfast in the morning. They went on a few dates, had sex a few more times, and then drifted apart.

The club, that tiny microcosm of busybodies, followed the saga of Kitty's virginity like a soap opera. The client who had offered $10,000 for Kitty's virginity found out that it was no longer in existence and called her a whore. That upset her.

"How does *not* selling sex make you a whore?" I ask when she comes crying into the dressing room after the incident.

That question startles her so much that she forgets to cry and laughs instead.

"Point him out to me," I tell her, and we huddle behind the curtain separating the dressing room from the main floor. She points to a man wearing a suit, who is in his mid-thirties with a receding hairline.

"What are you going to do?" she asks me.

"Teach him a lesson," I say and pull the curtain aside.

I march straight up to him. "Hi," I say. "I'm Star."

He looks at me uncertainly. "You're not my type, honey," he says, eyeing me up and down.

"It just so happens that you're not my type either," I shoot back. "Losers who call women sluts are a big turn off for me."

"All women are sluts," he snarls.

"I bet you don't get laid a lot." I eye him right back. "Or only when you pay."

"Who the fuck do you think you are?" he snorts.

"The person in charge," I say, and gesture to Donnie who lurks in the doorway like a wall of granite.

Donnie snaps to attention and makes his way over. "This asshole needs to go home," I say. "And preferably never come back."

Donnie's hand, approximately the size of a dinner plate, drops on the man's shoulder. He jumps.

"She started it!" he protests.

"And I'll end it," Donnie says placidly.

"You bitch!" the man shouts. "Getting a man to do your dirty work."

I recoil from the spittle that sprays across my cheeks and then recover and laugh in his face. "Oh, honey. If it were up to me, I'd put my stiletto through your temple." I pat him lightly on the shoulder, making him quiver with rage. "This big man here is protecting you!"

Donnie hauls him out, ignoring the stream of protests and profanities. Returning a minute later, dusting his hands together as though he'd touched something dirty, he asks me, "What was that about?"

"He called Kitty a whore."

Donnie shakes his head. "Only weak, insecure men insult women."

I lean against his shoulder and he puts his arm around me. "On that, big boy, you and I agree."

Chapter Thirteen

Couple's Therapy

Experienced customers sit at stage one because that's the dancer who determines the music. When we dance to music we choose, it's the best performance. In the two years I worked at this club the owner tried a couple of times to dictate the kinds of music we could play. As one of the more powerful performers at the club, I led a mutiny that finally ended his objections. I argued that my customers came to see me perform to my music and that stifling my creativity would negatively impact the tips I earned, losing money for the club. I'm persuasive. He caved.

One of my favorite sets pairs Eurythmics' "Sweet Dreams (Are Made of This)" with Marilyn Manson's remake of the same song. The first is peppy and upbeat, and the remake is dark and scary sexy. During the first song I wear a long, white jacket that glows and sparkles in the lights. Underneath the coat I wear white velvet shorts, and I tie my hair up with a white bandana. When the song changes I remove all of the white, letting my hair fall free, revealing a black studded thong. Light into darkness.

I'm on stage one. I've taken off the shorts and reach up and pull the bandana out. My hair falls in tousled curls down my back. I time the removal of the jacket to the crescendo of the song, and the woman sitting at the end of the stage claps, laughing. The man next to her runs his hand up her back affectionately.

I sink into the splits and then lie back, bringing my legs together sharply so that the heels of my shoes slam together. The woman jumps at the sound and laughs again.

I somersault backwards and then crawl toward them. The man lays a ten-dollar bill on the stage.

I ignore him and go for her, putting my hands on her shoulders, my hair tumbling down over hers, pulling her face within inches of my naked breasts, sparkling with sweat, glitter, and body spray. Sitting up on my knees, I pull her close enough that I feel her breath against my belly. Another ten appears next to the first. That's good enough money to pretty much ignore the other customers sitting at the stage.

At the end of the set I circle around to thank them.

"I'm Natasha," I say. "Thank you so much."

The woman turns toward me, smiling. "I'm Kim. This is Ken."

"Ken and Kim." I nod. "Got it. Well, Ken and Kim, feel free to have a drink with me later." I step away from the stage, but Kim doesn't take her eyes off me until I disappear into the dressing room.

"Couple at stage one," I warn Lila, who is changing for her next round on the main stage. I know that Lila doesn't like dancing for women. Bi-curious she is *not*.

"Ugh," she rolls her eyes. "Go get them before I get up there."

I drop my clothes and money on the counter and sit down to start facing all the bills the same way. I try to keep my money faced throughout the shift because it cuts down on time spent at the end of the night, when the club buys back dollar bills in exchange for larger denominations.

Bambie is curling her eyelashes at the mirror. "I don't get what you got against girls," she says to Lila.

"I'm not a lesbian," Lila retorts.

Bambie shakes her head. "Neither am I!" she shoots back. "But girls are fun."

"Heterosexual, homosexual, bisexual," I mutter. "Can't we just be sexual?"

"Amen," Bambie says.

"Yeah, well, I like dick," Lila snarls.

Lila is defensive about her inflexible heterosexuality. Personally, I find it kind of funny. "Fine," I say. "Your loss. They tip really well."

Lila just shoots me a sardonic glare.

I finish organizing my money and tuck it into the tiny lunchbox I carry as a purse. After refreshing my lipstick, I head to the bar to wait for Cutie to finish her set. When her last song ends, Lila is called to stage and I walk over to Ken and Kim, still occupying the same seats at the end of the stage.

I pull Kim's chair back and sit on her lap. She squeals in surprise and Ken laughs. "How about that drink?" I purr into her ear.

Ken gets up and holds out a hand to help me to my feet, then pulls Kim up with the other. Offering an arm to each of us, he escorts us to the bar as Lila takes the stage.

They order bottled beer and I order a mixed drink after waiting for Ken to ask me what I want. I am way past the novice mistake of ordering before I'm asked and then being stuck paying for my own cocktail.

"So," I ask, while our drinks are being prepared. "What brings the two of you in tonight?"

"Well, we recently moved here and we're looking for a new club," Ken tells me.

"And what are your thoughts so far?"

"Well," he grins and tips his beer bottle toward me. "You're pretty nice."

"We like it," Kim chimes in. "The girls are very pretty."

"Hot," Ken says, his eyes skating down my body.

I clink my glass against his bottle. "I think so, too." I gesture toward a table positioned midway between stage one and stage two. "Would you like to sit?"

A waitress comes over and talks Kim into ordering a round of shots. I order a kamikaze because it's easy to reduce the alcohol content without the customers noticing.

Kim is fixated on Lila. "She's so beautiful."

"Yes, she is," I agree.

Lila is one of the most beautiful women I have ever seen in person. She has naturally curly jet-black hair and skin so pale and flawless that she glows. She's thin and lean with pert breasts, narrow waist, and full hips. It's hard not to look at her.

"Unfortunately," I divulge, "she doesn't like girls." I do not feel like this is a betrayal; I'm saving her the embarrassment of having to tell customers herself. On a couple of occasions I have watched her perform for women, and if it wasn't so painfully hilarious, I would have felt badly for her.

Kim's face falls. "That is too bad."

"It is," I agree. "But luckily we can watch from over here."

"I feel bad watching without tipping."

My opinion of Kim goes up a notch. She gets it. "Ken can tip," I point out.

He lights up. "I can!" He roots hurriedly through his wallet. "Today it's good to be a man," he tells us and heads for the stage.

Kim and I watch Lila dance for him, enjoying the show as much as he does.

"I love to watch women dance for my man," Kim sighs.

I laugh. "And he obviously enjoys watching women dance for you!"

"Yeah," she says absentmindedly, her attention fixed on the show happening before us.

When Ken returns he's a bit flushed, and Kim grabs him by the shirt and kisses him passionately. I glance away, watching from the corner of my eye.

He's even more flushed when she releases him. "I think we need a private dance immediately," he says to me.

I finish my cocktail at a swallow and stand up. "Well, come on!"

It's technically against protocol, but I let Kim sit in Ken's lap instead of her own chair in the private dance area. I've been working here long enough now that management trusts me not to break state law even when I bend the rules of the club a little.

Another way I bend the rules is by getting entirely too close to Kim. Turning my back to them, I start my show by sitting neatly into a cross-legged position and then leaning back into her lap, making full contact against her body, my head against her breasts. I undulate slowly, my back between her legs, creating slow friction. Her body is pressed back into Ken.

I mostly dance for her, but I know that it turns Ken on. They get their money's worth. At the end of the set Kim's chest is splotchy and her eyes are dilated. Ken is a bit more composed but grinning from ear to ear.

"How much do we owe you?" Ken asks.

"It's $20 a song," I say, hoping that he gets that it's *per person*.

I do not need to worry. They're experienced customers. He hands me two twenties and a ten. I make the bills disappear; I try to keep the money mostly out of sight. I don't like to remind customers that ours is a financial relationship, and I also like to keep the customers' minds off how much they're spending.

"I need to go get changed for my next set," I say. "But Cody will be on stage two next, and I highly recommend being there. She's awesome."

"Thank you!" Kim says and reaches to hug me. I allow this, amused by how tightly she grips me.

As I walk away, they're making out in the chair. The bouncer gives me a questioning look and I hold up a finger, signaling that he should give them a minute before breaking them apart. Customers aren't supposed to stay in the private dance area if they're not getting a dance, but 50 bucks is worth a bit of leniency. I want them to have a good time. And come back.

They do come back. Once or twice a month they come in for an evening and buy a private dance with me and usually Cody and sometimes Trinity. They also tip well on stage and are well behaved, polite, and fun. They're also clearly very into each other, listening closely when the other speaks, obviously hot for one another, respectful of the other's preferences and desires. Sometimes they diverge in their taste for women, and one or the other will wander off in pursuit of a different dancer.

"Don't you get jealous?" Trinity inquires of Kim one evening when Ken has disappeared into the private area with Lila.

Kim laughs, sounding genuinely surprised. "Of course not! Ken is free to do whatever he likes."

Trinity is clearly baffled. I know that she's been married for several years and has a young daughter. She won't let her husband come to the club because she's afraid that he will look somewhere other than at her.

"But what if he cheats on you?" she asks Kim.

"He wouldn't do that," Kim says matter-of-factly. "If he wanted to have sex with someone else he'd tell me."

"What would you say?" Trinity asks, sounding horrified.

"I'd probably ask to watch!" Kim replies with a laugh. She sees the shock on Trinity's face and sobers. "In all seriousness, Ken and I have an agreement that, if one of us wants to have sex outside our relationship, we'll discuss it rationally."

Trinity turns to me. "What do you think about all this?"

"I think that it sounds perfectly reasonable. Communication is key in any relationship. And jealousy is lethal."

Trinity shakes her head. "Y'all are weird. I gotta go get ready for stage."

Watching her walk away, I say to Kim, "It always amazes me how strippers can be such prudes."

"In my experience, almost everyone is a prude," Kim says. "I find that strippers are usually a bit more sexually explorative than the rest of society, but puritanical attitudes still exist, even here."

Kim and Ken come into the club for their bachelor and bachelorette parties. They are finally tying the knot, and they bring all their friends in for the pre-ceremony celebration. We show them a good time.

For $60, a groom, or bride, or someone celebrating a birthday, can be brought onto stage to have three girls dance for him or her. Ken and Kim go together and choose Cody, Bambie, and myself to dance for them. We sit them back-to-back in straight chairs and make them sit on their hands to restrict any urges they might have to grab at us. The three of us rotate, a wall of female flesh.

As the second song starts, I kneel between Kim's legs and pull my halter top over my head. Flipping my hair forward over my face, I grind my head along her thigh, stopping just short of the juncture between her legs, teasing, simulating. Running my fingers along the tops of her legs, I pull her shirt out of her jeans, watching her face, making sure that I have permission. Slowly I pull her shirt up. Cody takes one of her hands and Bambie takes the other up over her head, and I pull her shirt up and off, revealing a lacy white bra and a smooth expanse of stomach. She laughs wildly and flushes. Ken cranes his head around to see. The crowd applauds and hoots. Money rains onto the stage.

Bambie leans her forward in the chair and unclasps her bra in one quick move. Kim flushes even more but lets us take it off, freeing full, heavy breasts. Pulling Cody and Bambie in on either side of me to hide my actions, I run my fingertips out along her collarbones and then very quickly down the slope of her breasts, brushing her nipples. The flush spreads along her chest, but it's no longer embarrassment.

I step back, smiling victoriously as we move back around toward Ken, who has been neglected. In addition to the money lining the stage, now shots have appeared, a whole row of them. The other customers in the club have wandered over to watch the show, and it's three deep around the stage.

Standing 3 feet above the crowd, the lights shimmering on my bare skin, I breathe it in, this surging sexual energy. I love the club like this, when everyone is having fun, the flirtation and playfulness of both the customers and the dancers filling the air. This feeling is so taboo in American culture and I wish that it wasn't. It's okay to exult in sexuality. It's fun to play and tease. It's empowering to disrupt social norms.

Of course, if this was generally acceptable, I couldn't make thousands of dollars engaging in the forbidden. Stripping is taboo and that's what makes it lucrative. I close my eyes and lean back into the feeling. Right now, in this moment, I am exactly where I want to be.

Chapter Fourteen

Black and Blue

Beside me, Tess sighs deeply, causing me to glance in her direction. We are alone in the dressing room, though soon it will begin to fill with dancers checking in for the night shift.

Tess stands naked in front of the mirror applying foundation to the bruise that I now notice spreads across her cheek. "What happened?" I inquire.

Her eyes meet mine in the mirror, and I see uneasily that she is on the verge of tears. I don't know her well; I keep most of my stripper colleagues at arm's length. I have just potentially opened a door that I will not be able to close. But the bruise is dark and angry.

She forces a smile. "Oh, you know. I deserved it."

No matter how many times I hear stories of abuse from women, the language they use always shocks me. I shake my head. "Nope. No one ever deserves to be hit. Ever."

Her eyes drop from mine and she fusses with the little pot of foundation. "You sound like someone who knows."

I puzzle over her words. Does she mean that I speak with conviction? Does she think that I have experienced being hit?

"My boyfriend threw a television at me once," I share finally. "I broke his nose."

She laughs, wiping her eyes. "I bet he really beat the shit out of you then!"

I shake my head again. "Of course not. I kicked him out of the house and broke up with him. Had the locks changed by that evening."

She looks at me in disbelief.

"As soon as someone is willing to use violence against their partner, it's over. Always." I go back to brushing foundation over my cheekbones.

"But you know what men are like."

I feel myself getting irritated. "Stupid boys have been getting away with violence against women for centuries because women rationalize it using shit logic like that," I snap.

Her eyes fill with tears again and I feel bad. I turn to face her. "Look, you have to learn to stand up for yourself."

Her chin trembles and she looks down. "I don't know how," she whispers.

I feel tightness spread across my chest. I am out of my depth here. I do not understand abuse or the mentality of the victim. No one has ever touched me with violence. Even the TV-throwing boyfriend did not so much throw it as knock it off the counter in my general direction. And the look of sheer misery on his face told me immediately that he had no intention of harming me. I still ended the relationship, though. I didn't want to give that miserable look a chance to grow into something else.

"Look." I reach out and take her hand. Her fingers close tightly over mine. "Men are just people. There are good ones and bad ones. And you can't allow yourself to stay with a bad man."

"But..." Her voice is no more than a whisper. I have to lean in to catch her words. "But he loves me."

"No." I give her hand a hard squeeze, then reach out and lift her face when she does not look up, forcing her to meet my eye. "Love is soft and caring and playful. Sometimes it's hard but it is never violent. It's normal to quarrel and struggle to communicate. But no one should ever hit. *Ever*."

"You hit your man."

She's got me there. "That's when I knew it was over," I reply finally. "I knew I couldn't stay in a relationship where that sort of thing had been introduced."

She is openly crying now and I hand her a tissue. "But they have all hit."

The tightness in my chest drops hard into my stomach.

I feel myself sway and grip the edge of the dressing counter. "All of them." I repeat her words, trying to make sense of what she's telling me. I think I know what she's telling me. "Everyone has always hit."

"Starting with your parents," I say. I'm not really guessing. I know this story.

"Yes," she whispers. "My mom used to..." She falters and then steadies herself. "My mom used to trade me for drugs."

Now I do sit down. But I keep holding her hand. "How old were you?"

She scrubs her eyes with the tissue and shakes her hair back, seeming to brace herself. "It started when I was six."

"Oh, my god." Now I am the one whispering. "Oh, Tess. I'm so sorry."

She meets my eyes. "You're saying that this never happened to you?"

"Nothing like that has ever happened to me."

She stares at me, seeming almost angry. "You're saying that no one has ever hit you."

"Never."

"And no one has ever molested you."

"No."

"Raped you."

I shake my head, mute.

She pulls her hand away. Taking one last swipe at her eyes, she says, "Well, aren't you lucky."

I'm stunned. She picks up the foundation and begins covering the bruise, working quickly and methodically.

"Tess..."

She glances at me in the mirror, her eyes hard. "What?"

"I am lucky," I say.

"You bet your ass you are."

I am silenced in the face of her anger. I have revealed myself to be a different sort of woman, one who does not fear men. I am an alien creature, dismissed as impossibly distant.

Studies reveal that a woman who has been sexually abused is almost twice as likely to be abused again. Abuse changes a person, makes them take more risks, normalizes assault. Maybe a person who has been raped is likelier to project victimhood, attracting predators.

I have always been fierce, a fighter. I communicate in no uncertain terms and demand respect. I was taught to make good choices and never settle for anything less than being seen as a human with autonomy.

But I am also lucky. Predators sometimes target women like me. I cannot take full responsibility for remaining unassaulted. It is good fortune and not anything I have done that has kept me safe from the lecherous uncle, the drunken frat boy, the creeper in the bar following me home.

Chapter Fifteen

The Addict

I stand at the bar sipping juice; the bartender blends orange, pineapple, and mango with just a little lime soda to make a sweet, bubbly cocktail. It is early in the night and the usual crowd of regulars are arriving to take their places at the bar. They will sip beer all night, teasing the dancers and ribbing one another about past transgressions, real and imagined. Only two stages are open and a couple of guys sit at each.

I hear the doorman talking to an arriving customer, and I glance back to check out the new arrival. The guy is young, baby-faced. He's got to be barely 21. He gives me a nod and a smile that looks slightly nervous. I smile back.

He takes his change and slips his wallet back into his jeans. Behind him the doorman gives me an imperceptible nod. Baby Face is loaded for business. The bouncers often see into customers' wallets and alert us when someone comes in carrying a lot of cash. My smile widens.

"Hi," I step forward, hand outstretched. "I'm Star."

"Jason." He gives my hand a shake.

"First time here?"

He's looking over my shoulder at the darkened club floor. Candy stretches out on stage one, her skin sparkling with glitter that we're not supposed to wear. The owner fears that customers' wives will wonder why they're coming home covered in body glitter and has banned its use. But we all break the rules.

"First time ever in a place like this," he says and shoots me the nervous smile again.

"Well, let's get you a drink," I say and lead him to the bar.

"Would you like anything?" he asks.

"Why yes, thank you. I'll have a seven and seven," I tell the bartender.

When he pays I glance quickly into his wallet. He has over $100 in twenties with a few smaller bills tucked in. He also has three credit cards lined up in the wallet's pockets. Two of them are platinum.

"Let's sit." I pick up our drinks and lead the way to a table just back from stage. Candy arches her back, looking at us upside down. I wiggle my fingers at her and she flicks her tongue playfully.

"So." I lean toward Jason, my breath in his ear and along his neck. "If you're a strip club virgin, what would you like to know?"

He's riveted by Candy's body laid out like a buffet. "Everything."

"I like the sound of that," I purr. "If you look, it's polite to tip." I nod toward Candy.

He flushes slightly and looks back at me, his eyes sliding quickly across my chest before meeting my gaze. "How much should I tip?"

"A dollar or two. If you sit at stage you should keep a dollar in front of you."

He peels a couple of bills off and hands them to me. "Can you show me?" He nods at the stage.

I stand and step to the stage, folding the money lengthwise and placing the dollars side by side. Candy rolls onto her stomach and rises to all fours, crawling across the stage to me. When she places her arms around my shoulders and pulls me into her breasts, I smell the bubblegum-scented body spray she favors. It's cloyingly sweet.

She pulls out the strap of her G-string a couple of inches and I slip the money in. She releases the elastic with a snap.

"Just like that," I say, sliding back into the seat next to him. Jason grins, and the flush on his neck is not embarrassment.

"It's also nice to tip a girl if she sits with you for a bit. And private dances are 20 a song."

"How much should I tip you?"

I bite back a grin. "Five bucks here and there is standard."

He slides a five across to me and I tuck it quickly into my shirt.

"I have to go get ready for stage," I tell him. "I expect to see you there."

"Yes, ma'am." He tips me a cocky little salute.

I walk back to the dressing room. I don't need to get ready for anything, but I figure I'll give him some time to eyeball Candy. I've told him the rules and got him primed; now I need to back off so that he doesn't think I'm greedy. Maintaining the illusion that we're all just here because we're into each other is key. If he decides that all strippers are materialistic, he'll leave. That will deprive me of the hundred bucks in his wallet.

I open my locker and scan through my outfits. I am wearing one of my early costumes; as the evening wears on my clothing becomes more and more elaborate. I quickly peel off the green dress I'm wearing and remove my leopard costume. It consists of a halter and micro shorts in a wonderful animal print. I don it quickly and switch out my heels for ankle-high platform boots with silver buckles.

Katrina glances up at me from where she's curling her hair at the mirror. "Got someone on the hook?"

"Maybe." I quickly freshen my lipstick just as I hear my name called to stage.

Over the course of the evening I ply Jason with drinks. Not enough to get him smashed but maintaining him good and tipsy. He visits the ATM twice after spending the cash he has. I make two bills off him and the rest of the girls do well. I convince him to tip $5 a song per dancer. Overall, he drops several hundred dollars.

I also learn that he's new to town. Originally, he's from Alabama and we spend a while sharing stories about the South.

He'd just graduated from the University of Alabama and had been headhunted by a local tech company. Fresh out of college he has a good job with plenty of potential to grow.

I tease him about his accent, and he responds by grilling me about why I don't have one. I tell him that it only comes out when I drink, and he orders me a refill.

I don't expect to see him again soon; the amount of money he's spent is significant. Even for a boy with a fresh, new job it's a welcome-to-town kind of splurge. He has a good time and I introduce him around to make him feel welcome. But he's young, decent-looking, and I figure that he'll quickly wind up with some nice girl who won't want him in strip clubs.

The next night, in he walks. Then the night after that. Then he's a regular.

He doesn't always spend big, but he always buys drinks for the dancers and tips a few of us well. But at least once a week he drops a grand or close to it.

I don't think that much about it initially. I know that he's sharing a house with a couple of guys and I know he makes good money. He spends a lot, but I figure he lives off noodle bowls the rest of the week. He drives a nice car that's several years old but reliable and fuel efficient. I assume that he's an adult and knows what he's doing.

For several weeks he hits on me relentlessly. He wants my number, to take me out, to buy me pretty things. I milk him for all he's worth, knowing that eventually he will figure out that I will never be his girlfriend. He buys me costumes and brings me jewelry. I promise but never deliver.

It all comes to a head one night after he's had one too many drinks.

"When will you go out with me?" he slurs for the thousandth time, putting an arm around my waist and pulling me close to him.

I push him away playfully. "I have exams right now. I have to study. So maybe next week?"

He pouts for a minute and then brightens. "But I'll see you at breakfast?"

He's become enough of a regular to get himself invited to breakfast after Saturday shift, when a bunch of the dancers, the bartenders, the DJ, and some of the bouncers go out for food. Several of the regulars come along as well. The local 24-hour café holds the backroom for us, and there's usually a group of 15 or 20 people.

"Yes," I tell him. "I'll sit with you."

He brightens a bit. "But we'll go out next week?"

Suddenly, I've had enough. He's grown on me. I feel affection for him like for a small, over-exuberant puppy. He's sweet and lonely in a new place, and all at once the money is no longer worth it. I watch him drink heavily three nights a week, and the amount of money he's spending has got to be above his means. I cannot lead him on anymore.

"Jason." I put my hand over his and gently turn him toward me. "I can't be your girlfriend. I'm sorry."

His lip trembles and I fear that he's drunk enough to cry. "Why not?" he asks plaintively.

"Because I don't date customers."

"Why not?" he asks again.

I try to explain it as briefly and directly as I can. "I don't mix my personal life with my job. I'm here to make money. That's it."

I have broken the stripper code, and the fantasy comes crashing down around him. But I don't let up.

"You're a nice person and I've really come to care about you. I think that you're drinking too much and I'm worried about where the money is coming from."

He turns away from me and darkly contemplates the maple wood of the bar. "I had an inheritance."

I wince at his use of the past tense. "How much of it have you spent?"

He sighs deeply enough to break my heart. "All of it."

"How much was there?" I'm hoping for a small number.

"Sixty thousand dollars. It was from my grandmother."

I feel a sinking sensation in my stomach. He'd been spending even more than I had allowed myself to believe. "You've spent 60 grand in four months." It's not a question but I have to vocalize it to wrap my head around it. I mentally calculate: that would be about $15,000 a month or $1200 three nights a week. Every night I'd taken several hundred, plus gifts and drinks. He regularly bought rounds for the girls and the regulars, and I wasn't the only girl he tipped generously.

"Jason." I make him look at me again. "You have to stop."

He swigs noisily from his glass. "But I love you. I love all of you."

"Jason." I repeat his name. "I know you think you love us. But none of this is real!" My gesture takes in the whole club. "This is a fantasy. Something to indulge in once a month or a few times a year. The people here aren't your friends."

His lip trembles again. "But you're so nice to me!"

I harden myself. "Only because you spend money."

His eyes do well up now. I take the glass out of his hand and tug him to the door. "Jason is ready to leave," I tell Dean the bouncer. "Get him a taxi."

Jason pulls away from me. "I can't leave my car. I have to work."

I grab a pen and write my cell number on his hand. "Call me tomorrow. I'll come get you and bring you to pick up your car."

He stares blearily at his hand. He now has in his possession what he's been trying to get for weeks. "I don't have cash for a cab. I gotta go to the ATM."

I peel $20 off the roll of cash in my purse and hand it to Dean. "Put him in a cab."

When Jason tries to resist one last time, Dean takes him firmly by the arm. Dean is 6 feet 5 inches and 250 pounds of muscle. No one resists Dean. "Fuck," I curse to myself watching the two of them walk out the door, Dean towering above Jason. A cab from the queue pulls forward and Dean dumps Jason unceremoniously in.

He rings me at two o'clock the following afternoon. He sounds sober and meek. "Can you take me to get my car?"

"Sure. Where do I pick you up?"

He's waiting for me on the front step when I pull up in front of his house. He is pale and shrunken in the bright afternoon, his eyes hidden behind dark glasses. "You're even prettier in the daylight," he tells me.

"Thank you," I say. Then, "Have you thought about what I said last night?" I'm not even sure he totally remembers.

"You said that none of you are my friends."

"Put your seatbelt on," I order and pull away from the curb.

He complies, childlike, saying nothing.

"That's right," I continue. "I said that we're not your friends. That doesn't mean that we don't like you; we do. But strippers make money off men. That's what we do. It's a job."

"So you kept telling me that you would go out with me so I'd give you more money."

I flinch internally. But I can't stop being honest now. "Yes."

He doesn't say anything else and I don't push him. When we pull up next to his car, sitting lonely in the vacant parking lot, he turns to me. I wait to see what he'll do.

"Thank you for telling me," he says.

"You're welcome," I reply.

"And thanks for the ride."

"Of course."

I leave him standing small and alone in the bright sunlight. I don't expect to see him again.

The next week when I walk in the door for my Saturday night shift, he's standing at the bar. Next to him stands Fate, a day-shift girl I don't know well. She's tall and voluptuous with the palest skin I've ever seen. Chestnut hair falls in thick waves to her waist. Her green eyes narrow at me.

"Star!" he cries and comes to hug me. I smell the alcohol on him, see it in his eyes.

I hug him back. "Hey, man. What's the haps?" I wonder how long he's been here today. A while, judging by his level of intoxication. Over his shoulder Dean rolls his eyes.

I pull away. "I have to go change for my shift. Good to see you."

That night Fate stays past shift change. I watch her with Jason in the private dance area. They're over there for a long time. Afterward, Dean pours him into another cab.

I continue to see him every weekend. Fate switches her shift to work nights. Now he comes only for her.

Over the next two months I determine that I don't really care for Fate. I don't let her see it though; I walk away a lot in this job in order to keep the peace. The other girls are more open in their disdain, and so Fate latches onto me because I don't treat her like total shit.

Here, there are day-shift girls and there are night-shift girls. Everyone starts working at least one day-shift; it's part of the hiring requirement. And there are a handful of girls who want to work days for whatever reason. Some of them go to night school; some work other jobs. Some have kids they like to put to bed. But most girls want to move to nights as soon as possible because the money is much better. Management determines who gets to work nights and it's all about earning potential. Looks are some of it, but personality and showmanship are part of it, too.

Fate is pretty, but she's not a real performer and she has an overdone, brassy quality that can only be described as "trashy." In a club that markets itself as high end, it's about class, not flash. Fate is all flash.

But Jason comes in at night and brings enough money with him to buy Fate onto the night shift. In addition to the money, the gifts pour in: clothes, shows, jewelry, and then one day a car.

That night, as she gloats over the new gift in the dressing room, I ask her bluntly, "Are you fucking him?" I had seen her the night before, standing with him at the bar, her hand rubbing softly along the front of his jeans.

She looks at me. "No," she says.

She seems so direct and matter-of-fact that I find it hard not to believe her. "But you give him hand jobs under the bar."

A flush rises along her cheekbones. "It was only once. And I just stroked him some. He didn't finish."

I shrug and go back to dotting glitter along my eyebrows. We rub up against customers all the time and claim that it's by accident. The line into intentional is slight. I don't really care, but I am curious. He is crashing and burning so spectacularly that I find it hard to look away.

A couple of days later he calls me in the middle of the afternoon. He's crying so hard that at first I can't understand him. Then the words come out more sensibly.

"I'm leaving," he says.

For a moment I fear that the emotional outburst is suicidal in nature and my heart takes a leap in my chest. "Where are you going?"

"Home."

Not any better. "To Alabama?" I clarify.

"Yes." He gulps and brings himself more under control. "My parents are here. They're packing me up. I snuck away to call you."

I consider a 22-year-old man "sneaking away" from his parents. "Do you want to go?" Given the hysterics I think it's a reasonable question.

"No!" It is a drawn-out cry.

"Where's Fate?" I ask.

That starts the sobbing again. "She doesn't love me."

"I could have told you that!"

My response startles him into silence and then he chuckles. It makes me feel much better to hear that little laugh. "You *did* tell me that."

"I did," I agree.

"She just used me and then dumped me when I ran out of money."

"I thought you were already out of money."

He pauses. I can't even hear him breathe.

"Jason? Where'd you get the money you've been living on? To buy that car?"

He sighs deeply. When he speaks again he sounds ten years older. "I embezzled it from the company I work for."

It's much worse than I would have imagined. "You *what*?"

"My dad paid off the company. But I'm $80,000 in debt to credit cards."

"Oh, Jason. How did this happen?"

"I don't know!" he wails and now he sounds like a toddler. "We had to meet with the owner of the company. He agreed not to press charges but I have to leave the state."

"You got lucky," I say. "You could be headed for jail."

"But I have to live with my parents!"

I laugh. I can't help it. "You're lucky you have parents who can bail you out."

"They're so mad."

"I bet! You spent, what? Close to $200,000 in six or seven months? You blew through an inheritance, stole from your place of employment, and ran up debt you'll be paying off for the next 20 years. Of course they're mad."

"I don't know how it happened." He pauses. "They're making me go to rehab."

"You probably need it."

"I thought you cared about me." Now he just sounds sulky.

I feel exasperation rising. "You know, I do care about you. But if we're being honest, I don't care that much." I hear a shocked inhalation. I continue, relentless. "I think you're a nice enough guy but you've been very, very stupid. People you can buy are not the people you want to be with."

"I bought *you*."

Now I'm angry. "No, you didn't. I took your money until I figured out that it was hurting you and then I walked away."

"But you didn't help me!"

"That is not my job. You did this all yourself."

He's silent.

"I wish you the best, Jason. I really, really do. I hope you learn from this." I wait to see if he's going to say anything. "Goodbye, Jason."

"Goodbye," he says.

Chapter Sixteen

The Female Gaze

The dancers are simultaneously in control because they watch
and are controlled because they are watched.
—Alexandra G. Murphy

Stripping is a violation of cultural norms and yet that was one
of the things that attracted me. I am, and have long been, an
intellectual. I am interested in what is considered forbidden. The
scholar Michel Foucault notes, in several of his works but most
notably in *Discipline and Punish*, that one cannot truly understand
a society without looking into its shadows, the places that the
culture says are taboo, off limits, dangerous, insane, morbid, or
disgusting. Sex work is the only industry in the world where
women consistently make more money than men, and there is a
reason that it is considered distasteful, and regulated or illegal.
Part of me loved making money through exploitation of the male
gaze. If patriarchy is going to objectify my body, then I am going
to benefit from that and use it to my advantage.

Another part of me grew profoundly aware of how women
are objectified, not just in gentlemen's clubs but in life. Strippers
report concern for their safety as being a high priority when
choosing a club and remaining satisfied at work (Maticka-
Tyndale et al. 2000; Bernard et al. 2003; Lilleston et al. 2012).
But all women are concerned for our safety. That's why we
walk through parking garages with our keys balled in our fists.
It's why we dial 9 and 1 on our phones when walking home
alone, finger hovering above that last digit. It's why we watch
our drinks at clubs and practice the buddy system at parties.
Contrary to popular opinion, I have been more afraid for my
safety walking along a public street than I ever was in a strip

club.

In the countless articles and books I have read by academics studying sex work, two points become apparent. First, many of the assumptions found in society regarding sex workers are also found in academia. Second, one assumption academics make is that sex work is not formally studied by many people. While the assumption itself is false, there are aspects of stripping that have not been studied: male experiences, the differences between different kinds of clubs, and the different attitudes between different dancers cross-correlated with race, educational background, work in other aspects of the sex industry, partnership status, parenthood; the list goes on.

Statistics often hide as much as they reveal, and academics seem as prone to getting it wrong as anyone else. Even researchers have biases, often unconscious, that influence what they study. For example, writing for *The American Journal of Public Health* (2012), Eva Moore, Jennifer Han, Christine Serio-Chapman, Cynthia Mobley, Catherine Watson, and Mishka Terplan conclude: "Young women in exotic dancing have an increased need for reproductive health services relative to women in other professions" (1833). This conclusion is based on a sample of 71 women in their "early twenties," 75% of whom reported that they had worked, or were working, as exotic dancers. Sixty percent were black and 33% were white, with negligible numbers of other ethnicities reported. The study was completed in downtown Baltimore, and the authors paid no attention to the impacts of race, class, educational attainments, or whether or not the young women who also made money in other areas of sex work were at higher risk than those who did not. The findings indicate that "61% of the dancers...reported...having sold sex" (ibid). The assumption drawn by the researchers is that high percentages of dancers also sell sex and are thus in need of reproductive care.

While it *may* be true that strippers are likelier to sell sex than the average 20-something, the extrapolation that *all* exotic dancers are thus at "high risk" is questionable and completely overlooks the different kinds of stripper. "Essentialist claims about the 'intrinsic' nature of sex work (whether oppressive or liberating) clash with the *variation* in sex work," notes Weitzer (3). Furthermore, 25% of the young women in the study did *not* work as exotic dancers, and the study did not include any information about these young women working in "other professions." This study is a prime example of researchers reading onto women's bodies what they assume they will find.

Researchers studying sex work often suffer from confirmation bias. It is notable that "[h]istorically, the opinions and experiences of sex workers have been consulted only when they confirmed (or could be used to confirm) one or the other partisan position... Missing from the literature...is any analysis of the temporal experience of stripping" (Barton 587). Lacking the first-person account, assumptions, yet again, are imposed on women's bodies, and our experiences are viewed through a contemporary, patriarchal lens that often overlooks the complexities of the job. When we read "the literature of radical feminists, we learn that dancers are all victims of sexual and physical abuse whose employment in the sex industry perpetuates patriarchal disdain for women" (Barton 586). I noted in the concluding chapter in Section I that some studies have highlighted that dancers come from dysfunctional families. But "dysfunction" is not defined nor is any comparison made with women from dysfunctional families who do not strip. Lastly, there are no percentages or any indication of the numbers of women working as strippers who come from functional family backgrounds. No cross-analyses of class background, educational level, or race exist to my knowledge.

Very few studies ask the women themselves, and those that do ethnographic work in strip clubs are often limited in scope and sample size. The varieties of experiences must be considered in order for anyone who does not have direct experience of this environment to begin to grapple with the complexities of this kind of work. Many authors draw conclusions that do not appear in the narratives they have collected.

One egregious offender is Andreas G. Philaretou in the article "Female Exotic Dancers: Intrapersonal and Interpersonal Perspectives" (2006). The author claims that female exotic dancers are "particularly vulnerable to developing chronic alienation and becoming overwhelmed by their pseudo-sexual selves at the expense of their real selves" (44). The findings are based upon *five* interviews done with dancers in five different clubs in three different states. My read of the excerpts of the interviews is that the dancers have a nuanced perception of the job that includes both positives and negatives. And yet the author concludes that the dancers must "acknowledge and rewrite their subjugated sexual narratives in more positive and empowered ways... Through self-reflection and re-narration, [female exotic dancers] can be enabled to mold their subjugated sexual narratives and proclaim themselves as sexually emancipated human beings" (48). While the author does acknowledge that club managers and owners can support healthy work environments by embracing dancer insights and listening to suggestions, ultimately the conclusion is that dancers are lying to themselves when they report finding aspects of their job empowering. This is a prime example of confirmation bias and completely overlooks much of what the dancers actually said. Strippers are considered unreliable narrators, but women's voices are often not believed in general.

An even more problematic claim appears in the article "Exotic Dancers: Gender Differences in Social Reaction, Subcultural Ties, and Conventional Support" by Constance Barton, Christen DeGabrielle, Lynette Cartier, Elizabeth Monk-Turner, Celestine Phil, Jennifer Sherwood, and Thomasena Tyree (2003). The authors suggest that dancers can develop rejecting attitudes toward men as a result of being constantly objectified. Thus, dancers are likelier than the rest of the population to develop bisexual and lesbian relationships. This perpetuates the very troubling idea that abusive relationships turn people into homosexuals. The article completely overlooks the environment of the club as experimental and potentially subversive and perpetuates the antiquated idea that orientation can develop in response to negative experiences with the opposite sex.

Many authors fear that dancers are at risk of sexual violence. However, *women* are often the victims of sexual and physical abuse, profession notwithstanding. The accepted statistic in the USA is that 1 in 3 to 1 in 5 (depending on the sources one accesses) women will suffer sexual assault in her lifetime. My guess is that this average will hold pretty true in the environment of strip clubs. If it is higher it will only be slightly higher. But I can't say for sure because no one has studied it. My point is that *no one* can say for sure because, again, the studies have not been done. As Moore et al. admit, "exotic dancers are a rarely studied subset of sex trade workers" (1833).

Ironically, however, the claim that there hasn't been much work on strippers is contradicted by Katherine Frank, who writes, "Authors often claim that the literature on exotic dance is sparse or that the subject is not taken seriously in academia... Yet even a cursory review turns up dozens of articles on these issues" (501). She goes on to include a bibliography with over a hundred articles and books. Yet, in spite of the plethora of studies, there are aspects of clubs and those who work in them that have never been studied. Rates of sexual assault among dancers as compared to the general population is just one example. I listed, above, several other aspects of the job that have not been studied. So, while there has been a lot of work done on strip club dancers, much of it is repetitive. There remains a huge domain for research that has not been touched.

Furthermore, strip clubs are not homogenous. There are

profound differences between clubs. They can be roughly divided into working-class clubs and high-end clubs (Barton 2002), but even this categorization obscures vast differences within each type. Dancers usually research different clubs in their areas in order to determine which club fits their needs. I certainly did and I spoke with many women who had done the same. We shared tips, experiences, and insights with one another in order to make informed decisions about where we wanted to work. Some clubs do have high numbers of employees who also work in other aspects of sex work: the pornography industry, prostitution and escort services, and so on. Other clubs pride themselves on being "clean" clubs where the use of hard drugs, prostitution, and other sorts of high-risk behaviors are minimal. The level of safety differs between clubs. Some clubs have open private dance areas that can be easily monitored by bouncers and security systems. Other clubs effectively put the dancer in a closed room with a customer, increasing the possibility of harm.

In the five years I worked as an exotic dancer I only know of one co-worker who prostituted herself. If others engaged in that sort of behavior, they kept it very discreet and out of the club. Prostitution was an offense resulting in immediate termination in the clubs I worked for. Customers who propositioned dancers violated state law and would be banned permanently. Furthermore, while alcohol and marijuana were consumed fairly openly, other drugs were frowned upon and also constituted fireable offenses if taken publically or abused. I knew one dancer who went off the rails on methamphetamine and was summarily fired. Some girls used a bit of cocaine, but they kept it off the radar.

The clubs I chose were safe; the women were in control. We were carefully monitored and our word was enough to get a misbehaving customer expelled. The parking lots were cleared at the end of the night and bouncers walked us to our cars. Often, local police patrolled the area during shift change and at closing.

Ultimately, what is missing from academia is a "female gaze." Dancers watch customers, each other, and ourselves. The club is paradox: we participate in our own objectification, but we do so with purpose and intention, subverting the very patriarchal environment that subjugates us. We form relationships with customers, men who buy the right to look, and these relationships are not "fake" because of the commercial transaction involved. We negotiate with managers and club owners so that employment is mutually beneficial and we feel safe in the club environment. We learn to frame negative experiences in order to learn that our worth is more than how we look, more than what we earn in an evening. The club is intersectional, and power and oppression traverse our bodies. It can be enormously humiliating. And it can be liberating. It is both.

Section III

The Abyss Gazes Back

The result of all the telling only deepens the enigma and makes woman's erotic force something that male storytelling can never quite explain or contain.
—Peter Brooks

Chapter Seventeen

The Cross-Dresser

Stage one is packed, Marilyn Manson blasting through the sound system. Every chair is full and the crowd is raucous. As the beat crescendos, strobe lights flash and money rains from the sky. A man sitting at the end of the stage places a folded five-dollar bill on the tip rail. I crawl toward him, my eyes locked on his. I see him swallow and lick his lips. In his eyes, I am the only thing that exists.

He is white, early fifties, with thick grey hair pulled back into a low ponytail and a matching grey beard. He looks like any average white, middle-aged, American male, little stomach pushing over his belt but otherwise fit. Except that he's wearing women's clothes.

Large glasses with pink frames cover his eyes; they are of the early 1980s style still favored by my grandmother. His blouse is a complementary peach paired with a mid-calf grey skirt, tan pantyhose, and low black heels. As I approach he slowly reaches up and unbuttons the blouse, one faux pearl button at a time, until I can see the top of a functional white bra. It's stuffed, pushing out the front of his shirt over a flat chest covered in grey hair.

My gaze never wavers, the small smile curling my lips widening slowly. But behind my seductive gaze my brain is whirling. I know that cross-dressers are almost exclusively cisgender, heterosexual men. Drag queens are of a different category entirely but cross-dressers are often assumed to be gay. I know that they're not, but I have never before encountered one. I'm powerfully curious.

I kneel before him, wearing only a G-string and heels. His eyes travel up my body, lingering on my belly, up over my breasts, to my face. He licks his lips again. I rotate my hips slowly and his gaze drops to the slow gyration of my pelvis. When I pull the string of my thong out, he places the five-dollar bill against my hip, conscientiously avoiding touching my skin.

Before I can move away, he peels a second five from the roll in his hand, but instead of placing it on the tip rail, he inserts it into the exposed edge of his bra. I laugh and he smiles back. We are not supposed to take money with anything other than our hand, and so I lean forward, placing a hand on either shoulder, bringing my chest close enough to feel his breath. Holding myself with one hand, I run a fingertip down his chest, covered in wiry grey hair, and under the top of the elastic. I feel him take a quick breath. Slipping the bill out of his blouse, I let my breath tickle his ear and then flip neatly backward, somersaulting away.

After my set I quickly skirt the stage, thanking the customers for the tips. The man still sits at stage, but he's tipped over $10 for a single set and so I pause and ask his name.

"Doug," he says and then gives a small shake of his head, as though correcting himself. "But can you call me Donna?"

"Donna." I hold out my hand and he shakes. I notice that his nails are carefully manicured and painted pale peach. "I'm Nora."

"I'm so pleased to make your acquaintance," he says.

"Likewise," I reply. "If you want to have a drink together later, let me know."

He glances at the stage where Bambi is working her magic. "After this set?"

"Sure," I say and step away. That stage is now the territory of another dancer and I try not to poach. I catch Bambi's eye and she tips her chin toward me. I lean in over the stage and she hugs me, her body against mine.

"What's up with the faggot?" she purrs in my ear, her hair hiding our exchange.

"He's not gay," I say, biting back irritation. "And he's loaded."

"Fair enough," she says and releases me.

I go to the bar and watch Bambi dance. I notice that she doesn't stay in front of Donna long; for each customer at the stage she performs for a minute or two depending on the size of the tip. With Donna she turns her back, twerks her butt, and moves on. He gets up and leaves halfway through her second song.

I give the waitress a nod and walk to the table he's taken against the wall with a good view of the stage action. "May I sit with you?" I inquire and he nods enthusiastically, leaping up to pull my chair out for me.

"So. Donna." I rest my chin on my hand, looking up at him coyly through my eyelashes. "I haven't seen you in here before."

"I haven't been in for a while. You're new."

"I am, I guess. I started a few months ago."

"You're so beautiful," he tells me.

"Thank you," I say. "I like your top." I don't, but flattery works a variety of magics.

His smile widens. "Thank you so much!"

I can tell that he's not complimented a lot.

"But do you think this color goes with grey?"

"Hmm." I narrow my eyes as I consider the outfit. "It depends on what you're going for. It's very office chic."

"Like what a secretary would wear." He nods, satisfied. "I think office girls are sexy."

"Are you an office girl?" I shoot him my best suggestive smile.

"Why?" He flutters his eyelashes coquettishly. "Do *you* think office girls are sexy?"

I laugh. "That depends on the office girl."

He laughs along with me and then returns to my question. "No, I am not an office girl. I'm a lawyer."

"Oh, I have a cousin in law," I say. I always try to make personal connections. "He likes it. What do you like about it?"

He considers. "I like helping people," he says finally. "I feel like I'm making some small contribution when I can really make people feel like someone's in their corner."

"That's beautiful," I reply honestly. "What kind of law do you practice?"

"Mostly workers' comp cases. People who have been jerked around by their employers after being injured—I like to help them get the care they need."

"Do you ever get people you think are lying? Or injured themselves out of real negligence?"

He shrugs slightly. "I find that most people are honest."

I nod. "I find that, too."

"Even working here?"

"What do you mean?"

"I just assumed..." He pauses, searching for the right words. "Don't men try to take advantage?"

I laugh. "Oh, yes. But they're honest about it! Most of the time they tell me exactly what they want, or what they want to do to me. Then I get to say yes or no."

"Then let me be honest with you." He leans across the table and takes my hand.

"Okay." I lean in, matching his serious tone.

"Do you have a gown? Something elegant?"

"I do."

"Can you change into it and give me a private dance?"

I grin. "Of course." He releases my hand and I stand. "I'll be right back."

In the dressing room I peel off the black vinyl micro skirt and crop top I'm wearing and root quickly through my locker for a floor-length gown in emerald velvet. Its halter top is crusted with rhinestones and a slit runs up one leg to my thigh. I pair it with a pair of patent pumps and silver bangle bracelets.

His eyes light up when he sees me. "That's perfect! You're so elegant."

I hardly think that skintight velvet qualifies as "elegant," but I keep my mouth shut. Stripper elegant, maybe.

I take him to the private dance section and sit on the edge of the small stage while he situates himself in the cushy chair clients sit in.

"May I ask you a question, Donna?" I ask.

"Shoot."

"What pronoun do you prefer?"

He positively glows at my question. "Thank you *so* much for asking!" he exclaims. "That is *so* thoughtful! I am a man and I identify as 'he.'"

"That's what I thought. But I wanted to be sure since you prefer a woman's name."

The next song begins and I begin my dance. I keep the gown on, seeing how his eyes are drawn more to the garment than my body. I play with the clothing, squatting, legs apart, so that the slit gapes open, flashing the rhinestones on the velvet thong I wear underneath, untying the straps but letting the top ride low on my breasts while still covering me. Only at the very end do I let the dress glide down my body to puddle on the floor at my feet.

When the music ends, Donna claps long and hard. "That was wonderful!" he gushes.

I'm amused and touched by his appreciation. I'm getting the feeling that he needs to feel seen for who he really is.

"May I have another dance?" he asks, handing me a 20-dollar bill.

I check the dancers on stage. "I have to go to stage here in a bit." His face falls. "But right after?"

"Yes! That's great." He takes my hand again. "Thank you."

"For what?"

When he looks shyly back up at me, I meet his eyes steadily.

"For taking me seriously."

"Lots of people don't?"

He shrugs and looks down. I see his chin quiver. "I come here because most people don't treat me any different than anyone else. But only some of the girls will dance for me. And some guys threatened to beat me up in the parking lot once."

"That's awful." I give his hand a squeeze.

He glances at me very quickly and I see tears in his eyes. "It's okay. Donnie came and rescued me."

I glance at the door where Donnie lurks, a hulking figure of at least 300 pounds of muscle. My opinion of him goes up. "Good for Donnie."

He lets go of my hand and swipes his eyes furtively. "I just want to wear pretty things."

I pick up the green velvet. "So do I."

Two months later Donna asks me to go shopping with him. I'm always cautious about accepting invitations to meet customers outside of the club, and so I ask "Shopping for what?" to buy myself time to think.

He's holding my hand, gently stroking my lacquered nails the way he likes to do. I think he likes to see his polished nails next to mine.

"Clothes," he says. "You have such wonderful taste."

I wonder why he thinks that, given that all he ever sees is stripper clothes. While what I wear in the club is a partial reflection of my personality, my wardrobe is a careful presentation of the femme fatale to appeal to my mostly male clientele. Red catsuits and schoolgirl skirts are not what I wear grocery shopping.

"You want me to take you shopping for women's clothing?" I'm still baffled. His style, what he wears to the club, can only be described as "liberal granny": sandals with white socks, tweed pantsuits, sweater sets.

"Yes!" He squeezes my hand. "I need to update my look."

"What do you have in mind?"

"Just take me wherever you go."

I shop mostly in thrift stores and Hot Topic. I don't think it's what he has in mind.

"Where do you shop now?"

"JCPenney catalog."

That explains it. I think quickly. "Dillard's?" I finally suggest. They have edgier items while retaining modest sensibility. Plus, I need a dress for a family reunion and maybe he'll spring for it if I agree to take him.

"I'll go wherever you say."

We make plans to meet at a local mall.

Getting dressed to meet Donna takes some planning on my part. He's cast me as a fashion icon without ever seeing how I really dress. And how I usually dress to go to class or run errands is jeans, a tank top, and flip-flops with my hair piled on top of my head. I don't want him to see me and realize that he's made a terrible mistake.

I settle on skinny black jeans, motorcycle boots, and a babydoll T-shirt with "goddess" written on it in red glitter paint. I brush the makeup on heavier than usual but lighter than I wear at the club, foregoing the black eye makeup and dark lipstick. I twist my hair up into an elegant roll on top of my head.

I meet Donna in front of the mall at 11 a.m. I've never seen him dressed like a man, and it takes me a minute to recognize him in jeans and a white T-shirt. He looks grandfatherly with his white beard and little potbelly.

He greets me by telling me how beautiful I look and kissing me dryly on the cheek.

"So, Don," I say, shortening the name he asked me to call him to a male moniker. "What are we shopping for?"

"What I really want is a ball gown. With all the accessories. And shoes!" His eyes light up. "But I'm not good in heels."

"You got it. Let's start at Dillard's and work from there."

I'm a little concerned about his body shape in dresses. He really is shaped like a middle-aged man, as opposed to a middle-aged woman. He turns down my initial selections as being too frumpy. He wants sexy.

I flip quickly through the plus-sized selections and find a floor-length gown in deep blue satin. It hangs almost straight from rhinestone shoulder clasps, and I like the weight of the fabric and the cut.

Donna looks at me doubtfully.

"I think it will hang really well," I explain. "The fabric will cling just enough to make you feel really alluring and move with your body. I think you should try it on."

At that, Donna looks truly alarmed. "I can't."

"What do you mean?"

"I mean..." he stumbles. "I can't go in the men's dressing room with that. And they won't let me in the women's."

"Ooooohhhh." I clearly haven't thought through this whole cross-dressing thing. "Give me a minute. Stay here."

I make my way quickly out of the women's section and go over to lingerie. The sales clerk is a friendly-looking woman in her mid-sixties. She looks nice enough and there are no customers around.

"Excuse me," I say. "I have a bit of a problem and I could use your help."

She smiles warmly. "How may I assist?"

I don't beat around the bush. "I have a friend. A male friend. He likes to wear women's clothing." I pause to gauge her response.

"That is a bit unusual," she says. Her expression stays blank and warm. "What seems to be the issue?"

"He can't try on clothing in the men's room because...well... it can be dangerous for him. And he can't go in the women's room for obvious reasons. So he has to buy things, take them home, try them on, and then return items that don't work."

She narrows her eyes thoughtfully. "You know, I think I have just the thing."

"Yeah?"

"We have a handicapped changing room that's unisex. Just around the corner here. Bring your friend over and I'll take care of you."

I grin. "Thank you. Thank you so much."

She smiles primly. "It's really no trouble at all."

I think that Donna is going to hug me when I tell him the news. He takes the sapphire gown from me and insists on trying an orange sundress with an empire waist. I think it will make him look like a pregnant orange, but whatever.

I'm right: the floor-length blue hangs over his figure in a flattering line. His wide shoulders and hairy arms look a bit odd but I'm getting used to that.

I select lacy panties (loose in the crotch area), a matching bra, and stockings with a garter belt. We hit jewelry next for a rhinestone choker and clip-on faux diamond earrings. Finding pumps with a low heel in his size is a bit difficult, but we finally agree on a pair of Mary Janes that aren't awful.

Under the bemused eye of the sales clerk we also buy a whole array of skirts and tops in modern prints and fabrics. She rings everything up without ever losing her cool little smile. At the end of the transaction I ask for her card.

"If my friend comes in alone in the future, will you help him?" I ask.

"Of course," she replies.

"Just don't let him buy anything peach or orange," I say. "Hideous with his complexion."

She laughs merrily and Donna shrugs with a small embarrassed smile. "That's why I brought you," he says.

That Friday, Donna arrives in the full sapphire ensemble. I tell him that he looks fabulous.

Chapter Eighteen

Rain

I sit with a customer at a table one row back from stage. He tells me that his name is Brad and that he's a long-haul trucker. Every month his route brings him through town.

I listen with half an ear, nodding at the appropriate places. What I'm really doing is watching Rain.

She is my complete opposite. On stage she wears cutoffs so short that they're almost a thong, the tattered edges cupping her ass like a lover, red G-string flashing when she bends over. She has a flannel shirt tied up high on her stomach; the sleeves have been cut off so that the sides of her breasts flash tantalizingly in the lights. She is tan, golden, with thick brown hair spilling down her back in loose waves. She dances to "country pop" and white trash metal: Garth Brooks, Kid Rock, Nickelback.

She's the hottest thing I've ever seen.

She has just started at the club. She's danced in Birmingham and Atlanta. Now she's here. She is bubbly, her mood contagious, making me laugh in spite of myself. She is completely without inhibition, stripping naked, exulting in her body.

"Do you like her?" Brad asks.

I jerk out of my reverie. I have forgotten about him. I glance at him, gauging his facial expression. If I say the wrong thing, I'll lose his money. Is he the sort of man who likes it when girls like other girls? Or is he threatened by that?

"She just started," I say. "I think she's beautiful."

"Not as beautiful as you," Brad says and takes my hand, rubbing his thumb lightly over my wrist. I want to jerk my hand away and wipe it against my skirt.

Instead, I smile at him, lowering my chin to peer up through my lashes. "Thank you. That's very sweet."

"You can go ask her to come sit with us when she gets off stage."

"Yeah? You'd like that?"

"Very much."

"Okay." I get up and leave him, signaling the waitress to see if he needs another beer. His is getting low and men with several drinks in them tend to tip more.

Backstage, Rain drops her clothes in a pile on the dressing counter. Dollar bills spill off onto the floor. She's sweaty, her skin gleaming.

"Good set?" I ask.

"We'll see."

She starts scooping up the money, and I lean down to pick up the scattered cash on the floor. I straighten the wadded bills, automatically facing them so that all the money is oriented in the same direction. I count 15 and she has another pile that she's also flattening and organizing. I see a five.

"I'm sitting with someone who invited you to join us?" It comes out as a question, though I didn't mean for it to.

"Yeah?" Now I have her full attention and she turns to face me. Her lips curve like a doll's, the lower a bit fuller. Her eyes are green, the pupils rimmed by a lighter gold. "He worth the time?"

"He tipped me $20 on stage and now he's paying $5 a song."

"Sweet! Thanks, girl." She hits me on the shoulder. "I'll be right out." She starts pulling on the shorts.

I return to find that Brad is halfway through his next beer. I slide into the seat next to him and purr into his ear, "She said that she'll be happy to join us. She'll be right out."

Instead of pulling up her own chair, Rain slides into my lap. She smells of clean skin and sweat and musky body spray. I slide my arms around her waist and rest my cheek against her back.

Rain leans toward Brad and her breasts strain at her bikini top. His eyes drift from her mouth, glossy with lipstick, to her cleavage.

"You didn't tip me on stage, now did you?" Her voice is pure Southern drawl.

"He was busy looking at me," I offer. We never make a client feel bad or even hint at something that might cause them shame.

"Well, let's fix that right up." He pulls his wallet from his back pocket and flips it open.

My eyes slither quickly over the bills. They are large denominations, and, while there are not a lot of them, there's about $300 in his wallet. This is a good sign, as men often take out the amount of cash they plan to spend before arriving at the club. It's way easier to take cash a man already has than get him to go to the ATM and pay our $6 withdrawal fee to get more. I slip the doorman an extra $5 every night; in exchange he tips me off to the men who come in with wallets bulging. Brad had earned a nod in my direction.

By the time Brad looks up to slide a five-dollar bill across to Rain my eyes are safely on his face. The illusion that it's all about him, not his money, must be maintained.

For the next couple of hours he is exclusively the property of Rain and myself. He sits at stage when one of us is on, and the other sits glued to his side encouraging him to tip. In between our sets we sit at a small table tucked cozily in a corner, ordering drink after drink.

Ours are served basically alcohol free with just a tiny drop of vodka floating on top; sometimes customers check to see if the drinks they're paying for have alcohol in them. The vodka is typically enough to fool them without intoxicating us. The tiny bit of alcohol also serves as a mild diuretic; over the course of an evening a girl might consume as many as 10 or 15 glasses of juice and soda. While we do sweat some of it out on stage, customers ply us with drinks, leading to overhydration. The alcohol helps.

By 1 a.m. Brad is very lubricated. Luckily, he's a sweet, sloppy drunk and we're all telling stories and roaring with laughter.

Rain tells a story about a time in Atlanta when she had found a wallet dropped by a customer. Upon returning it to him, the grateful man had emptied the contents, a whopping $500, into her hands.

I have no idea if this is a true story. It illustrates that Rain is not in it for the money, casting her as the stripper with a heart of gold. Customers eat this up and Brad is no different, patting her hands and telling her how kind and generous she is, how she deserved the reward.

I tell the story about the time I had skewered the hand of an overly aggressive customer with the metal heel of my shoe. Brad swears to protect me with undying devotion.

"Hey, I have an idea," Rain says suddenly.

"What's that?"

"I think we should celebrate this wonderful evening with a private dance."

Brad is not too drunk to ask, "How much does that cost?"

"Twenty dollars apiece," Rain says, leaning toward him, holding his gaze. Her lips part. I want to laugh but don't.

"Great idea!" Brad responds promptly.

I catch Rain's eye and she shrugs imperceptibly. He'd agreed very fast, and she should have set the price higher.

We order another round and escort him into the private dance area, which consists of a long couch with screens strategically placed to separate the dancers and give customers an illusion of intimacy. While state law forbids touching between customers and dancers when the girl is topless, here we push the limits of the law. While our clothes are on, we can climb all over the customer and we take advantage of the loophole to give the customer his money's worth.

Rain climbs into Brad's lap and purrs in his ear. I face away and lean forward slowly so that the skirt I wear climbs up my thighs. In a full forward bend I place my face between my knees and look up at them upside down. Rain laughs and slaps me on the ass hard enough to leave a handprint.

"Hey!" I protest, standing abruptly. I wrap my arms around her waist and pull her off of Brad. She protests demurely and mock wrestles me. I wrap my leg around hers and trip her, easing her to the floor and pinning her. She squeals and wiggles. I exert more effort in holding her down. We are face to face, lip to lip, and I smell the juice on her breath, the fruit scent of her lip gloss. We writhe, ostensibly for Brad's benefit. I enjoy the feel of her skin against mine.

At the end of the song we detangle, breathless and giggling. Brad looks at us, his previous mirth replaced by drunken righteousness. He flings two twenties down at my feet. I gape at him in astonishment, not understanding the sudden shift in his demeanor.

"Fucking dykes," he spits at me and storms off, staggering slightly.

I am speechless, my mouth hanging open. Rain stoops and scoops up the money. Handing me a twenty she says, "Well, it's a good thing we took all his money before." She turns and yells after him, "Faggot!" She rolls her eyes at me. "Asshole. Real men like girl-on-girl."

I wince at her cavalier words and take the money.

"We should go dancing!" Rain flings herself at me, wrapping her arms around my waist and pulling me into her. "Fun, right? I'll bring Trevor and you can bring Gabe."

I feel her breath in my ear and along my neck. Thoughts of Gabe, who I am intermittently dating, cease to exist.

"Yes," I say. "When?"

"Let's take next Saturday off." She breaks away and takes my hands, jumping up and down in excitement. "Yay! This will be so fun."

"Saturday's my money night," I protest.

She swipes at me playfully. "Who cares? You can afford it."

The next Saturday Gabe and I meet Rain and Trevor at the club and pile into their car to head out. I've never met her boyfriend, though she's met mine. Gabe comes into the club sometimes and works as a bartender at another club in town.

Trevor is average-looking: just under 6 feet tall, broad shouldered, brown shaggy hair, brown eyes. He wears jeans and a flannel shirt with cowboy boots.

Gabe is also in jeans but with motorcycle boots and a black button-down. They shake hands affably.

I wear a velvet catsuit with knee-high go-go boots and a spiked dog collar. Rain wears a denim miniskirt with stiletto heels and a white oxford tied just below her breasts, leaving her tan midriff exposed.

We arrive at the nightclub and park. The club is huge: enormous dance floor, three bars, lots of cushy chairs and couches. The seating areas are dim and lit with red and black lights. The dance floor pulses with lights.

"I forgot my ID," I tell the doorman, pouting. Gabe flashes his club badge. All the clubs in town issue their paid employees club badges so they get in free at any of the other clubs.

The doorman waves us in. I make a beeline toward the dance floor.

I love to dance. Stripping is one thing, but dancing, my body in motion to the music, is another. I miss dancing like this, just me and the pounding beat. Everything else fades.

Gabe and Trevor take a spot at the bar. They're manly men and don't dance.

Rain comes to join me. She loves to dance as much as I do, and we lose ourselves in the music, spinning and twisting and writhing.

We've arrived early and for a while it's only us. Then the floor begins to fill in.

The drinks keep coming. I don't usually drink much, and I pace myself but it goes to my head. The lights blur. I spin, a manifestation of sound.

Tan arms around my shoulders, mingled sweat, breath in my ear, along my throat, in my face. Our bodies move in perfect rhythm to the pulsing beat. Twice, men try to shove between us and we push them away. "I have a boyfriend," Rain tells one. "You're not my type," I say to another.

I am vaguely aware that we have attracted a crowd, but I am used to having eyes on me. I am more aware of Rain's body, her breasts against mine, her arms around my neck, the feel of her tight skirt against my leg. I hear only the beat of the music.

Suddenly there's a hand on my arm, firm and insistent. "Hey!" I say, pulling away. I look up into the stern eyes of a bouncer.

My first thought is that they've decided to boot me because I'm underage. But his other hand grips Rain by the elbow. He reaches back for me and leads us off the dance floor.

I play it casual. "What's up?" I inquire.

"The two of you can't dance together," he says over the music.

"What?" I have no idea what he's talking about. I struggle to make sense of his words through the liquor and the adrenaline rush of the music and Rain's skin.

"What the hell are you talking about?" Rain takes a more aggressive approach.

"We don't allow that lesbian shit in here," he says.

I gape at him, too surprised to respond.

Rain is less tongue-tied. "We're not lesbians! Look!" She gestures to Gabe and Trevor who are making their way toward us. "Boyfriends!"

"What's going on?" Gabe puts his arm possessively around my shoulder and I shrug it off.

"This dude says we can't dance together," I explain.

"Why the hell not?" Gabe inquires.

"We don't allow girl-on-girl here. This is a clean club."

"Who cares? It's hot!" Trevor exclaims.

I feel a rush of irritation. This isn't about him, isn't about what turns him on. I should be able to dance with whomever I please in any way that I want. "We weren't doing anything," I say. "We were just dancing. Just like all them." I gesture to the dance floor that is now packed. Some couples dance together, but there's a lot of free form going on as well, clusters of women and other mixed groups.

"You were dancing *together*," the bouncer explains, making a gesture to indicate our two bodies. He sounds out of patience.

"So?" I still don't understand. "We weren't making out. We're not naked."

Now he's done with us. "You need to leave."

"Now, wait a minute," Gabe begins.

But I cut him off. "Fine." I grab Rain by the hand. "We're going."

"Asshole!" she yells over her shoulder as I hustle her along. Trevor and Gabe trail after us.

In the parking lot I laugh with disbelief. "What was that all about?"

"Two chicks together *is* hot," Rain says petulantly. "Them's a bunch of faggots."

"Don't use that word," I tell her.

"Why not? That's what they is!"

I look at her. She's as beautiful as ever and I feel hunger for her perfect, smooth skin. But I begin to see that she's as bigoted as the bouncer who just kicked us to the curb.

"Let's go," I tell Gabe. "I want to go home."

Chapter Nineteen

Pretty Boy

It is early on a Friday night and the club is dead. Only one stage is open and I dance with myself, loosening up my muscles, getting into the groove. The DJ has played something slow and sensual and I slide down the pole, arcing my back, stretching. I become aware that a group of three guys is coming in, paying, showing their IDs. I watch them because there's nothing else to watch.

They go to the bar and I turn away, falling smoothly into the splits, warming up my hamstrings. In the mirrored wall of the club, I see them get beers, clink their bottles together. I lie down on my back and thrust my hips up, rotating my joints slowly.

They make their way over to the stage and sit down in a row. No money immediately appears and I roll onto my belly, rising to all fours to check them out.

The one in the middle makes my stomach flip. He is everything I like, and my first thought, immediate and irrepressible, is *I want that*. He is beautiful, the kind of guy you'd see in the movies, so perfect that it's hard to look away.

Like most people, I have a type. When it comes to men, I like them dark, swarthy. I like men who look like pirates.

This man has dark hair curling over his collar in ringlets and tightly groomed facial hair with a neatly trimmed goatee and long sideburns with a narrow strip cut just above his jaw, rockabilly style. The narrow strip of beard directly under his lower lip is colored fuchsia. His head is covered by a black bandana tied to keep his hair out of his eyes. He wears jeans and the most fantastic black leather biker jacket that I have ever seen: it is absolutely covered in spikes and safety pins. On one finger, the middle of his right hand, he wears a jointed ring that extends from his top knuckle to almost his fingertip. It's like my rings.

I fall immediately in lust.

I am not looking for commitment, or anything serious. In fact, I am not looking at all. But this boy...this boy is *yum*.

I go to him first. He's in the middle but I can't resist. I want to get a closer look. In an attempt to be fair I lie down and stretch out in front of all of them, one leg bent with my foot on the floor, the other out long. I watch him watch me.

His eyes are dark, framed by thick, curling lashes. He's not afraid to look and his eyes skim down my body, hesitating at the swell of my breasts, scanning down my legs, and landing on the V of black material between my legs, tight across my hipbones. That's where he looks the longest and then his eyes meet mine. I smile seductively.

His lips part slightly and he softens around the eyes but his expression barely changes. He is enigma, hard to read.

I sit up and pull the strap of my thong out. When he places the dollar in the strap, I notice his hands. Narrow fingers, clean nails kept a little long, fine-boned and masculine.

I love men's hands.

Off stage I go to the dressing room and dump a pile of clothes and money onto the dressing room counter.

"Oh, my god," I say to Kris who sits curling her hair at the dressing table. "There is the most beautiful man out there."

"Really?" She looks up with interest.

"Yes. He looks like Johnny Depp."

"No way."

"Seriously. Like 90s Johnny Depp. Like *Cry-Baby*."

Now Kitten is listening, too. "Okay, I'm going to look."

Kris puts down the iron. "Where is he?"

"Sitting at stage."

The two of them go out, mock wrestling at the door to get through first. It's early in the night and slow. A hot guy makes things more interesting.

I straighten my money and put it in my purse. I'm standing

at my locker trying to decide what to wear when they burst back in, giggling.

"You mean the one with the dark hair who looks like a pirate?"

"That would be him," I say, pulling out a black studded bikini. It's an outfit I usually reserve for later in the evening, but special times call for special measures.

"Yep." Kris picks up her curling iron to finish her hair. "You are not lying."

Kitten fans herself theatrically. "I'm up on that stage next. Ooh, baby." She paints bright red lipstick on her mouth.

I feel a stab of what I can only classify as jealousy. Kitten is total punk rock with bright purple spiked hair, a tattoo of a pinup girl on each bicep, and a safety pin through her ear. She might be pretty boy's type.

I quickly pull on the bikini and thigh-high black vinyl boots. I take a wrap of sheer fabric and tie it around my waist. I switch out the necklace I wear for a choker of silver spikes.

I follow Kitten out and feel relief when I see the three of them get up from stage as Jet switches places with Kitten.

"Aw, don't leave, boys!" she calls coyly.

"Just getting a refill," one of them says, holding up an empty bottle.

I follow them to the bar.

"Hi," I say, pushing between one of them and the pretty boy. "I'm Lex."

I shake each of their hands in turn. "Greg," says the pretty boy.

"Pleased to meet you." I hold his hand a fraction of a second longer.

They don't offer to buy me a drink but I don't take it personally. "First time here?"

"First time in a strip club," says the blond friend.

"No way!" I laugh. "Strip club virgins."

Greg responds. I have a hard time taking my eyes off of his

mouth. Now I know what people mean when they refer to lips as "Cupid's bow."

"We were just sitting around like we always do and someone said 'strip club.' None of us have been," he tells me.

"Well, what do you think?" I ask coyly.

"Naked women and booze?" the dark-haired friend says. "What's not to like?"

Greg's eyes are on Kitten who sits on the tip rail and has one foot on either side of a customer whose eyes are level with her nipples. "What's not to like?" he repeats.

One of my regulars comes in and I catch his eye. "Have fun, boys," I say. "I'll come check on you later." I run one fingertip down the row of safety pins on Greg's jacketed arm. "Nice jacket," I toss over my shoulder.

A couple of hours later they're playing pool in the smoking lounge. Every song, one or the other will put a dollar up on the stage in there, but they're pretty engrossed in the game. Kitten is sitting on the wide drink rail that runs around the wall behind the pool table. She is clearly trying to get pretty boy's attention and he does reply when she speaks, but mostly he's engrossed in the game.

As he lines up to take a shot, Kitten jumps down and sets her ass over the pocket he's aiming for. He laughs but doesn't hesitate and takes the shot. He lines up for another. He's concentrating hard and doesn't see me walk up behind him. Just as he shoots, I drag my fingernail lightly down his arm.

He misses. Curses. Laughs.

I walk away, glancing into the mirrors lining the walls to make sure he's watching me but too fast for him to see me look.

He's watching.

I can't get a read on him. He comes in every weekend after that, with a rotating group of five or six friends. They are all smart, funny, sweet guys, and they quickly make friends with the regulars, the staff, and the dancers. But pretty boy is a little more aloof, a bit watchful.

His mystery breeds rampant rumors among the dancers, who speculate endlessly about him. We discover that he's in cosmetology school, that he drives a Trans Am. He gives us makeup tips and gifts me eyeliner, probably still the most interesting present I have ever received from a man. It's really good eyeliner, too, and I throw away what I've been using.

I decide that he's a player. He has to know how good-looking he is, and the way his dark eyes look steadily into mine speaks of a cool confidence, knowing that I will come to him. He will wait, then use me and discard me. I try to decide if that's what I want.

Finally, one night the whole staff of the club is at breakfast and pretty boy and his friends are there in a booth together. One of them is on his knees, turned around in the booth, talking to Trinity in the next booth over. Greg throws a French fry at one of his friends and they all howl with laughter.

I get up from where I'm sitting with a couple of the bouncers and make my way over. His eyes rise to meet mine and his lips curve up slightly. His eyes are incredibly dark, even in the bright light of the diner. Not a hair is out of place and his swarthy skin has a natural, healthy rosy glow. He looks like he's been airbrushed.

"Do you want to meet me after breakfast?" I ask.

"Sure," he replies and my stomach does a slow flip.

His friends have fallen silent, and one of them pauses with a fork halfway to his mouth.

"Where should I meet you?" he asks.

I name a street corner downtown. I am not ready for him to know where I live. I still need to get a closer read of him.

"I'll be there."

"As will I." I turn and walk away, feeling my heartbeat hammer in my chest.

"Dude," I hear one of his friends exclaim. "Why is it always you?"

"Of course it's always him," another one of his friends says. "He's got what all the ladies like."

"What? A pretty face?"

"That goes a long way."

I file this conversation away. It seems to be proof that he does get a lot of tail. So he probably knows how amazing-looking he is. Which means that he's probably a player. I'm not sure I care; it's not like I'm looking for anything serious.

Main Street is dead at three o'clock in the morning. I sit in a doorway and wait, enjoying the night air. He pulls up in an early 1980s Trans Am that's custom painted with a dragon uncoiling on the hood. It's a wild car and it fits him perfectly. In many ways he is as theatrical as I am. The car, the elaborate facial hair, the fuchsia color in his goatee, the spiked leather jacket: every part of him is intentional, produced. Just like me.

I let him look for a minute before stepping out of the shadows. I don't wait for him to greet me but tilt my head down the street. "Let's walk."

He falls into step beside me. And we walk.

We walk until dawn streaks the eastern sky. We talk about the club, about friends, about movies we like and books we've read. I begin to relax. He does not make a single move toward me. He doesn't even try to take my hand.

I fall into bed as the sun comes up, feeling more confused than ever. I have met my share of players, and most of them make a move once they think the girl is on the hook. He didn't. So maybe he's not a player. Or maybe he doesn't like me.

The next weekend they're back and he greets me with a slow smile. "What are you doing Sunday night?" he asks.

"Not a thing," I say.

"Want to meet me again?"

I don't hesitate. "Name the place."

He names off a grocery store in a town several miles from the town where I live and work. "Meet me in the parking lot. Eight o'clock?"

"I'll see you there."

I'm a few minutes late because I can't find the store. When I pull into the parking lot he's leaning against the side of his car, smoking. My stomach does its slow flip. He looks like he should be on a movie set. It's kind of ridiculous.

"Get in," he tells me, and I tuck myself into the low-slung seat of the car. He heads up into the mountains, driving well and confidently. Just like he seems to do everything else.

I don't ask where we're going, just enjoy the ride. The stereo plays quietly and he doesn't speak, seeming engrossed with the curvy road unspooling in the headlights. He's comfortable in silence.

Several miles out of town he turns off onto a dirt road that switchbacks and then ends at a breathtaking drop overlooking the plains. Lights sparkle into the distance, mirroring the cloudless sky above.

I get out of the car and walk to the edge. He leans against the hood behind me and lights another cigarette.

"This is beautiful," I say.

He says nothing but I see him nod. The dim radiance from the lights below, the stars above, and a rising moon light his features, gilding his cheekbones and flashing in his eyes.

"I bet you bring all the girls here." I'm testing him, trying to break the smooth façade of his expressionless face.

"I bring friends here," he replies. "People I like."

I walk back toward him, trying to read his expression. "Do you like me?"

His voice softens. "Very much."

I walk up close to him, my body brushing his. Still he does

not move. He's sitting against the hood, his hands at his sides, open palms against the nose of the dragon painted on the car. I take another step, forcing him to move his legs. I step into the space between his knees. He regards me calmly, and I take in his perfect skin, curling eyelashes, parted lips.

I put my hands on his shoulders and still he does not move. He only watches. But when I lean in to kiss him he kisses me back. It is only when I press my body fully against his that one hand rises to my back, pulling me in, caressing fingers along my spine through the thin fabric of my T-shirt.

When I pull away he lets me go, his hand returning to the hood of the car. I sit next to him, my mind a welter of confused thoughts. I still don't have a bead on him. Then he takes my hand, his fingers curling gently around mine.

In the weeks, months, then finally years, to come I learn that Greg is exactly what he appears to be, nothing more and nothing less. He is aware of his beauty but only because people tell him. He mostly discounts it, though he does take pride in how he looks. His quiet confidence is exactly what it seems and was born through contemplation and teaching himself to be self-assured and honest. He is occasionally prone to shock-value behavior, like putting a cigarette out on his tongue. He is a calm, rational person with just enough wild to interest me.

Eleven months later we go to the courthouse and get married. As of this writing 17 years later, we are still living happily ever after.

Chapter Twenty

The Renaissance Man

I hang out in the smoking room a lot because that's where the pool table is. I don't really play pool, but the regulars do and I like to pass time with them when the club is slow or I need a break. I've been working here for only a few weeks, and already I've gotten to know the handful of men who come in almost every night to play pool, drink beer, and give each other shit. They don't tip, but they also don't proposition me or try to be my boyfriend.

I've noticed the man before, last weekend, and here he is again. He sits in the corner surrounded by a handful of girls. He tips $5 a song to some of the girls who dance on the narrow stage in the smokers' room, and I've seen him in the private dance area. He's maybe in his fifties, with elaborately groomed facial hair; this is what initially catches my attention. He's also immaculately dressed in pressed white shirts, linen trousers, and expensive sports jackets. On the pinkie of one hand he wears a gold ring with a darkly red flashing stone the size of my thumbnail.

At first I take him for a rich perv, but some of the experienced dancers, women I consider smart and thoughtful, sit with him. Finally I ask Kris, whom I trust, "What's up with the guy in the corner?"

She gives me a sly look with her dark eyes. "Come on over. I'll introduce you."

I narrow my eyes at her. "Very mysterious."

She shoots me a tight smile. "He'll like you. But he usually won't talk to a new girl without an introduction."

"Are you serious?"

She just tips her head for me to follow. Which I do. I love a good mystery.

As we approach the table, I see the man's head bent attentively toward Bobbie. "And what is your argument that Kierkegaard was the first existentialist?" I hear him ask. I can't hear her murmured response.

"'The paradox is the passion of thought, and the thinker without the paradox is like the lover without passion...'" I quote.

He looks up and regards me with light hazel eyes. "'...a mediocre fellow,'" we finish together.

He stands and holds out a hand for me to shake. "And *who* are *you*?" he inquires.

"I'm Lex." I take his hand and he encloses my fingers with a firm, dry grip.

"Of course you are," he says, his eyes sparkling. He places his left hand on his chest and executes a prim little bow, his mouth stopping just short of my hand. I feel his breath feather across my skin. "And I am Rodney."

"I'm very pleased to make your acquaintance."

"And I am most pleased to make yours, I'm sure. Any woman who can quote Kierkegaard has my heart for eternity." He releases my hand and flips one of the chairs at a neighboring table around. "Please, sit. You as well, Kris?" He turns his gaze to her and she smiles, a rarity for her.

"In a bit. I'm with a regular right now."

"Ah, yes." His hand rises to his heart again. "Well, we shall all pine for you in your absence." He looks at Bobbie and me. "Ladies? Will we not?"

I drop dramatically into the chair. "I am breathless until your return," I say, the back of my hand to my forehead.

Kris positively giggles and smacks me with her purse as she walks away.

I sit up and return to the interrupted conversation. "Now, is someone making the argument that Kierkegaard isn't the first existentialist?"

Bobbie shoots me a very tiny glare. It's clear that I've encroached on her territory and I smile at her reassuringly. I am not here to make enemies.

"Well," says Rodney. "Bobbie is taking a philosophy class and she says that her professor labeled Kierkegaard the father of existentialism. Then I asked, upon what grounds? After all, the man wrote almost a hundred years before existentialism proper."

I hesitate. I don't want to steal this conversation from Bobbie.

"Well, when I think of existentialism I think of Sartre. And Camus," she says.

"Yes. The French." Rodney nods thoughtfully. "And what do you think? Lex." He says my name deliberately, marking me, recognizing me.

The force of his gaze is powerful. The whole club seems to fade into the background under his regard. The opportunity for a real conversation about real things intoxicates me. Who is the seducer here?

"I think it depends on how you define existentialism," I say.

"Very interesting." He strokes his neat little goatee thoughtfully. "And how would *you* define it?"

"Well, I think there are two main characteristics. The first is the absolute belief in human freedom and responsibility. The second is a recognition of the absurd."

"Okay," Bobbie says, jumping forcefully in. "So by those criteria, was Kierkegaard an existentialist?"

"Personally, I do think so," I say carefully. "That quote about paradox as the passion of thought seems to me to be a profound recognition of the absurdity of life. The paradox is that which thought itself cannot think and yet we are compelled to pursue the unthinkable. That's pretty absurd."

"And what about freedom?" Rodney asks. "How do you read Kierkegaard there?"

"That's a bit trickier," I admit. "In 'Philosophical Fragments' he seems so deeply rooted in post-Reformation thought that free will seems to be part of the way he explains our pursuit of knowledge. But in the 'Teleological Suspension of the Ethical' he may suggest that ethics cannot be rational but is superseded by faith." I shrug. "But I've never entirely understood that piece so I might be wrong."

Rodney gazes at me, rapt. His eyes never leave mine. Bobbie fidgets, running her fingertip slowly over her lips. That's always a ploy to get attention. I'm stealing her thunder.

"At the very least," I say, "I think it's undeniable that his thinking influenced later thinkers like Sartre."

"And don't forget the Russians!" Rodney says.

I laugh. "Never. Dostoyevsky forever!"

Rodney turns his attention back to Bobbie. "If Lex will excuse us, I do believe that you owe me a private dance, young lady."

"Of course!" I leap to my feet, taking the cue to leave. "It was wonderful meeting you, Rodney."

He stands and executes that perfect little bow again. "Please join me again. I want to hear your opinion on a feminist reading of Plato's cave."

I blink at him, amazed. Who *is* this guy? He's clearly trying not to be Kierkegaard's mediocre fellow, but part of me suspects that we are all mediocre, at least sometimes. The passion drives us to pursue even unknowable knowledge, like true connection with other humans, and we always fall short. Therein lies the existential paradox. So many of my experiences in strip clubs revolve around people trying to connect. For pleasure, for money, for sex, for friendship, for simple human companionship. Rodney thrived on intellectual exchanges surrounded by the tawdry costumes, the stink of intermingled body sprays, the hustle of naked flesh in exchange for paper our society has deemed valuable. If that's not delightfully absurd, I don't know what is.

The night after meeting him for the first time I notice him arrive and hurry back to see him. Kris has beaten me, but she gestures toward another seat and I slip in next to her.

"I prefer the tragedies to the comedies," she's saying. "Hamlet's realization that it was all for naught, Juliet waking to find her ploy gone horribly wrong."

Rodney takes a sip of his brandy. "I love the use of masks and concealed and revealed identities most in his comedies."

"Shakespearean tragedies use the same device," Kris counters.

Rodney turns his penetrating gaze on me. "What do you think?"

I hesitate. He'd seemed so impressed with me the night before and I don't want to admit that I don't know a lot about Shakespeare. But I also can't fake it with him; he'll know I'm bullshitting quicker than a teacher reading an essay. I opt for honesty.

"Kris is the Shakespeare expert in this place," I say. "Though, to return to our conversation of last night, there's an existential absurdity to much of the great bard."

"You've read Shakespeare?" Rodney queries.

"Um…in high school."

Now Kris looks as astonished as Rodney.

"It's not my area!" I protest. I feel my cheeks grow warm. I am not used to having my intelligence questioned. In fact, I'm used to being the smartest person in the room. "I can't be an expert in everything!"

Rodney nods. "A valid point," he concedes.

"But Shakespeare is so…so…" Kris searches for a grandiose enough word. "*Excellent.*"

I shrug. "Honestly, I am not one of the people who gets him. I tried. I enjoy performances of his plays, but reading him just feels like a constant reminder that forcing everything into iambic pentameter just usually sounds stilted."

They both look at me with such horror that I can't help but laugh. "But ask me about how the *Ramayana* reinforces patriarchal ideals and I'm your woman."

Rodney looks back at Kris. "What do you think? Should we let her stay?"

Kris rolls her eyes. "I *suppose*. But only because I've been wanting to ask someone about why India has such a rich goddess culture and yet treats actual women so badly." She sits forward and crosses her hands attentively like a good student.

Rodney turns to me, fascinated. "That is a *most* excellent question. Please. Enlighten us."

I look back and forth between the two of them. "Okay. But then you have to tell me about your favorite Shakespeare play and why you like it best."

"Deal," they chorus.

And that is how I found myself discussing Indian religious history surrounded by naked women and the clatter of pool balls.

I have a hard time asking for private dances. Some girls are really good at it, but I struggle to find a way that preserves the fantasy that we're all here to have fun times at a naked party. I feel fake asking.

Rodney saves me the trouble and asks me himself. It's the third night I've sat with him.

"Of course!" I say relieved. "Right after my next set?"

"Come and get me when you're ready," he replies.

I dance my next set on stage two, on the main floor, and then hurry to the dressing room to change into something I think he'll like. He hasn't batted an eyelash at the metal and chains I'm known for wearing, but I want a more sophisticated look for him. I also don't want to look like I'm trying too hard. Stripping is like dating but more difficult. Dating is about getting to know someone. Stripping is about *pretending* to get to know someone. More specifically, it's about revealing certain aspects of self while hiding others.

I select a floor-length velvet skirt with a slit high up one leg and a halter top in matching deep blue. I pair it with a rhinestone choker and black patent heels with crisscrossing ankle straps. I strip off the studded leather bracelets I wear on each wrist but leave my signature silver rings in place.

Rodney doesn't say anything when he sees the outfit change. I don't know if I'm exasperated or relieved. He's playing me, and I'm used to being the player. He sees how intoxicating actual conversation is to me, and I recognize that he's using my intelligence to court my interest. But he's still the one with the cash. His ability to converse on a wide variety of topics does not change the fact that I am taking my clothes off for his money.

I take him to the private dance area and go into my show. He nods his head to the beat, a small smile playing on his lips. His eyes are intent and he looks mostly into my eyes. His forthright regard unnerves me a little and so I break his gaze by turning my back.

The existential paradox is that it is impossible to ever really know a person; we can never live in another's skin and inhabit their mind. Stripping is the paradox writ large: my essential self coated in layers of artifice and yet used so that I do not seem a shell. My self repurposed, exposed only in calculated ways. But isn't this the truth of all life? It's just harder to lie about it in the club.

Rodney shifts his eyes to catch my gaze in the mirror. Though he does look at my body his gaze quickly returns to my face. What kind of connection is he seeking?

Søren Kierkegaard died young at 42 years old. The son of a wealthy father and the household maid, he lived a life of privilege, walking the streets of Copenhagen, writing in his journal, and publishing philosophic tracts. I have long suspected that psychological angst and existential crises are First World problems experienced by those with privilege. Kierkegaard exemplified the "modern man" plagued by doubts, anxieties, and phobias. Never married, he appeared incapable of forming deep connections with others; his broken engagement to Regine Olsen remains a matter of speculation and seems to epitomize his inability to overcome personal uncertainties in order to maintain deep relationships with other people.

In the months to come I will discover that Rodney has never married and lives an extraordinarily solitary life. Virtually his only social interaction is with his employees, his invalid sister, and strippers. Though he jests amiably with the other regulars, often seeming to genuinely like them, he counts none of them as friends. He seems incapable of having relationships that dissolve power dynamics.

I lie down on my back and gaze at him upside down. The smile stays on his lips and I meet his eyes. He holds my stare, unflinching. I smile back at him and his expression does not change at all, only the small smile and cool regard.

We can either respond to the existential realization of absurdity by accepting our limitations as fact and working to overcome reality with communication and empathy, or we can accept ourselves as isolated and inhabiting only our own minds. The best of us, in my opinion, attempt to do both, delving deep into self-reflection while seeking increasingly sophisticated ways to bridge the gap between ourselves and others.

When I remove the top and skirt, Rodney glances at my breasts and then his eyes skate quickly down my legs. But then his gaze is back on my face, his expression gently bemused, as though he is laughing at the farcicality of the scene. I mirror his smirk back at him and he grins at me. We are co-conspirators of the absurd.

When the dance is over Rodney stands and thanks me with his small bow, and hands me double the price of a dance.

"Thank you," I say.

"Thank *you*," he replies.

The next night I feel more confident and ask him for a private dance immediately. If I spend time with him early then I'll have time for my regular who will arrive a bit later.

"Not tonight," he says, glancing up at me. He's engrossed by something Nikki is saying and his eyes immediately return to her. He barely pays me any attention at all, and after a few minutes of being ignored, I wander off into the dressing room.

Kris is curling her long, black hair, striking poses at herself in the mirror.

I sink down into the chair at my spot along the long counter that serves as a dressing table. "I think I did something wrong and pissed Rodney off," I say.

She glances over at me. "Why do you think that?"

"Last night he asked for a private dance and tonight he just told me 'no' and barely looked at me!"

To my surprise, she laughs. "I doubt you pissed him off. See if he tips you when you dance the smoking lounge."

"Then...why did he treat me that way?"

She sets the hot iron on the counter and turns to face me. "Rodney has a group of girls he likes," she explains. "You know, the smart ones."

I nod.

"He rotates through us, giving each girl a dance each night."

"Ohhhh," I say slowly.

"Currently, there are five or six of us that he's paying attention to, so your night will come up every third weekend or so."

I recalculate my monetary assumptions. I can't count on a dance every night but I can count on his stage tips.

"He's really kind of perfect," Kris is saying. "You have plenty of time to give attention to your more high-maintenance guys and still count on him."

"Got it." I stand up and start peeling out of the elegant outfit I'd put on for him. I'm glad that I understand the rules. It amuses me that he has a stable of women. He tries to play the intellectual, but he's still gratified to be surrounded by beautiful, young female flesh.

Rodney comes in almost every Friday and Saturday night. He arrives between 8.30 and 9 p.m. and is always dressed immaculately, not a hair out of place. He takes his place in the corner of the smoking room; if someone is sitting in his seat, he sits as close as possible to "his" spot and waits for them to move. Often, a dancer comes over and gently relocates the interloper. He chain-smokes to the point that I wonder how his lungs survive but limits himself to two small glasses of brandy. The bartender keeps a very good bottle in stock just for him.

He only favors girls who he considers smart and capable of keeping up with his conversation. He shows no preference for physical appearance or educational attainment; his preferences tend toward the college girls but only because we're likelier to be able to converse with him. He is equally stimulated by Kris, with her easy elegance and simple style; Kitty, who dresses like a baby doll in lace and satin; Bobbie, older than us at 30 and a little on the trashy side with her feathered bangs and spandex; or me, in spikes and leather. We are nothing alike on the outside, but all of us are quick-witted, capable of talking art, history, philosophy, and science.

Every time "his" girls appear on the smoking-lounge stage, he tips them $5 a song but never sits at stage. He buys drinks for everyone sitting at his table, including other regulars who often wander over to say "Hi." I can't keep track of how much money he spends but it's a lot. However, he favors a different one of the girls each night. Most of the time when my night is up he buys a single dance but pays double. Sometimes he buys two dances and still pays double for each one.

I've known him for three or four months when he suddenly turns to me and says, "I have tickets to *A Midsummer Night's Dream* next Sunday. Didn't you admit to enjoying Shakespeare's plays?"

"Yes," I say. "I'm the one who watches Shakespeare but doesn't read him."

"And you defended yourself so eloquently on that point that I cannot hold it against you."

I smile, wondering how to handle this turn of events.

"I would be most honored if you would accompany me," he continues. "We can have dinner beforehand." He lists the name of a very posh restaurant.

"That should work," I say, buying myself time. "Let me just go and check my calendar to make sure I don't have anything I'm forgetting about."

"Of course. I await your response."

I hurry to the dressing room and am relieved to find Bobbie changing clothes.

"Rodney just asked me to a play," I say without preamble.

She glances over her shoulder at me. "Go," she says with a shrug.

"He's okay?" I verify.

"Yes. I've gone out with him a couple times. I know Kris has. He's harmless."

"Thank you," I say gratefully.

"Don't mention it," she says, pulling a complicated neon orange strappy dress over her head. "That artsy fartsy crap isn't my bag."

"It's totally mine!" I exclaim.

I hurry back to Rodney's table. "Yes," I tell him. "I can go."

"Excellent. I would like to meet you at the restaurant and then I'll drive from there. Is that acceptable?"

"Yes," I repeat. "That's perfect."

I discover that the play will be outdoors. This complicates clothes a little, as I have to dress for potential uneven ground and elements. I settle on a tight but stretchy skirt, black with a white Chinese dragon picked out in embroidery. I pair it with a black, lacy tank top and silver sandals. Over the whole thing I throw a silver pashmina. I also pack an umbrella and light coat.

For makeup I go light but dramatic, with sweeping cat's-eye eyeliner, glittery shadow, and dark pink on the lips. Upswept hair with loose curls on top completes the look. I hesitate over jewelry and then settle on two jointed silver rings but no spikes.

Rodney waits in front of the restaurant and opens the door for me with a flourish. Our table is waiting inside, and I'm careful to order a single glass of white wine of medium price from the extensive list. I'm also careful to order food that's easy to eat and not likely to drip or get stuck in my teeth. It's just like a date but not a date.

Rodney eats with gusto and the conversation pauses as we both savor the flavors set before us.

"There's a reason this place has a good reputation," I say, closing my eyes to better examine the profile of contrasting tastes in my mouth. "I can never get the flavors to layer like this."

"You like to cook?"

"I do," I admit. "I've always loved to cook. Grocery shopping is one of my favorite things." I pause to consider. "Provided that I can shop with no regard for prices."

"I don't imagine you have to worry about that," Rodney says.

"I don't." I smile at him. "My job allows me to buy good food, pursue an education, and wear pretty things."

He raises his glass. "Here's to pretty things."

I clink my glass against his. This lifestyle can't last forever; I don't want it to last forever. I want to be a grown-up one day, with a career, and a forever home. I don't want to have to be strategic about whom I tell about how I make money. I'm not ashamed about what I do for a living but sometimes it's too much trouble to explain. Sometimes people require me to defend my choices and I'm not always up for that. Just like sometimes I'm not up for telling people my politics or religious choices.

The research on exotic dancers suggests that strippers are

always on stage in the sense that we constantly manage people's impressions of us. We manage what customers see, but we also manage our private lives, choosing to divulge what we do to some people and hide it from others. Academics think this makes our lives wrought by tensions and contradictions. They argue that we either burn out or begin to self-medicate in order to deal with the stress that comes from constantly managing who perceives us and how.

I don't think the academics get it. (I am one now so I can say that.) Women, and to some extent all people, manage how others see them. Everyone has secrets that they keep. Sometimes it's because these secrets cause shame, but often it's because we all deserve, even need, privacy. Some argue that it's exhausting to keep secrets, but that's because they've misunderstood secrets for lies. I have never been ashamed of being a stripper. My understanding of myself evolved, continues to evolve, but that doesn't mean that I regret who I was. Or who I became. And being careful about whom I tell has nothing to do with being guilty about who I am. Some dancers and ex-dancers may feel that way but I do not.

I share some of this with Rodney over dinner that night. He listens closely and then says, "It seems to me that humans have entirely too much entitlement and too many expectations of one another."

"What do you mean?"

"We're all constantly trying to get to know one another. Then, when we think we know a person and we find out something new about them, particularly if it's something we find shameful or startling, we feel betrayed. Like they lied to us."

"But, in some deeply ontological sense, do we ever know one another?"

He takes a long swallow of wine. "Everyone dies alone," he says finally.

I'm following his thinking. "We can never truly know another person."

He looks up at me, his eyes shining in the candlelight. "But that's okay," he says. "Because it's so much fun to try!"

I laugh. "There's that paradox again."

He leans toward me in the candlelight. "Don't you find that stripping is the supreme paradox?"

I think about it. "Yes," I say finally. "But so much of being a woman is rooted in the existential contradiction of what it means to be human."

He gestures expansively. "Continue."

"I am a biological entity with a particular experience of physical reality," I explain. "But culture writes expectations onto my body that shape my perception of myself. My very potential. These expectations concern the color of my skin, my sexual expression, my intellect. Due to the limitations of biology, I can never truly know what it is like to be another person."

"The Cartesian crisis," Rodney murmurs.

I nod. "This problem is exacerbated by the constraints that this society puts on me as a woman. I am supposed to be chaste and demure. I am certainly not supposed to take my clothes off for money. And I'm absolutely not supposed to enjoy it."

"Do you enjoy it?" The flickering light casts shadows across his expression.

I hesitate. He's getting off on this, I can tell. He has women playing to his intellect and also taking off their clothes. But I decide not to care. I'm getting off on this, too.

"Sometimes," I answer honestly. "A lot of the time. Sure, there are aspects of the job that aren't fun but most of the time..." I laugh. "Most of the time it's a blast."

I worked at this club for two years and I learned a lot about Rodney. I went out with him many times, to plays, the opera, a couple of book readings, the symphony. He worked as the CEO of his own tech company, hence the money. He lived with, and cared for, his invalid sister. He also lived with three cats, but they weren't allowed in his study because he smoked in there.

In spite of his regular appearances at a strip club, he struck me as very asexual. He enjoyed watching, liked when I dressed up to appear on his arm, but he never made even the slightest advance toward me. His sexuality was voyeuristic. Like in his beloved Shakespearean plays, he loved getting behind the masks of the strippers he courted and yet he seemed fully aware that all he would ever find is another mask. We were beautiful actors on his set and he moved us, and removed us, at will.

When I got married, I told him and he treated me no differently. In fact, he approached my spouse, who often came in to play pool and shoot the shit with the regulars, and shook his hand in congratulations. Then he invited me to a performance of *Madame Butterfly*.

I think Rodney loved finery. He loved beauty and surrounded himself with fine alcohol, good books, deep conversation, gorgeous women, interesting men, a nice car, gourmet food, and cigarettes. He embraced the paradox of being. Anyone or anything that fit his aesthetic was welcome. But he limited his relationships to those he could control, never opening himself to vulnerability.

Women are trapped in the dialectic of the male gaze. Our value so often lies in their regard. Rodney was the paradox: his esteem trapped me in my own need to be recognized as an intellectual and it freed me, transforming me into my sexual self. This is the passion of thought.

Chapter Twenty-One

This Is My Body Moving Electric

The rhythm is a pulse, driving me on. Lights on my skin, flickering sweat. My thoughts stop. There is only music.

Here on the stage I embody sexuality. Power lives in my veins, in the lines muscles make under my skin. I feel like anarchy, like broken taboos, like liminal space. I feel like god.

Dance is an act of creation. In the beginning, the Greek goddess Euronome danced the world into being. The great Hindu sagas are still told in dance all over India. Dance is often related to the female, a manifestation of her creative power. Sexuality is a metaphor for the act of creation, and thus dance, sexuality, and the ability to bring forth life became overdetermined representations of woman.

Dance is magic. It is a powerful visualization technique. It weaves spells both for the dancer and for the viewer. Dance unites the performer and the audience and is thus a symbol of sexual congress, the most intimate physical unification of bodies.

Around the stage is a wall of pressing bodies. Men, and a few women, laugh and cheer and throw money. Bills coat the stage. One of my regulars shoulders through the crowd and holds out a folded rectangle of money. I step to the edge of the stage and pull out the strap of my T-bar, meeting his eyes, which crinkle in appreciation. "You're beautiful," he says. I throw back my head and laugh. He slips $100 into the outstretched band of elastic.

I lie down on my back and stretch out. Hands appear in the air above me and dollars rain down. In ten minutes I make $1000.

It is my birthday celebration. For six weeks leading up to the day when I celebrate turning 23, I pass out business-sized cards that I have had made. On one side is a photo of my breasts with my fingers, sheathed in spiked rings that are hinged with my knuckles, crossed over them. On the other side is the date of my party and the information that the holder of the card will get into the club free on the night in question. All the club's regulars are in attendance plus a healthy smattering of men who have used my card to gain free admission to the local gentlemen's club.

Right now, they are all here for me. The other stages are closed, so for the duration of two songs it is all only about me. The clothes I remove are custom made specially for the occasion. There's a chocolate cake lit by candles for me to blow out at the end of the set. The piles of money are swept from the stage into a garbage bag.

It is the last time I appear naked on stage. At 23 I retire from stripping in order to utilize my master's degree and enter teaching, the vocation that will become my permanent profession.

In the coming years I will achieve tenure, a doctorate, and a critical feminist lens partially shaped by my years as a stripper. I will write this book, documenting my experiences. Twenty years later I still sometimes dream of the stage. I hear a certain song and it all comes rushing back: the smell of the club, the thrill of the taboo. My body begins to move, electric.

Chapter Twenty-Two

Athena, Stripped

Are women "active agents in their own oppression" (Murphy 327)? I'll leave that for the readers to decide.

I have told the stories contained in this book as accurately as I can. I did not engage in intentional ethnography while a dancer. I viewed my job as a way to make money that was lucrative, easy, fit my night-owl hours, and worked with my school schedule. However, I did pay attention. I kept a journal off and on, and recorded my thoughts, observations, and experiences. The observational work on strip clubs that has been done to date has been done by mostly female researchers who, if they strip themselves, typically do so for a single night or weekend. The other literature is memoir by dancers themselves who are not trained researchers and write for a popular audience. I am both: I worked as a stripper for a significant amount of time and I am an academic. Thus my observations are rooted deeply in my lived experiences, but I bring a methodological frame to my account. While I changed identifying details in order to obscure the identities of the people involved and while some of the people represented here are composites, these stories are true as I experienced them. The only person who is represented with complete accuracy is my spouse, Greg, and he gave his permission for me to write the segment about how we met.

I have tried to honestly represent myself in these pages, including my naiveté, vanity, and occasional unkindness. The reader is free to pass whatever judgments they may upon my actions and insights. In no way do I mean for this narrative to be definitive of the entirety of the world of strip clubs. I was not an academic when I became a stripper. I was a junior in college with no sense of my educational future. As I have stated on several occasions, I am white, well educated, and privileged in multiple ways. I cannot speak for all women who choose to take their clothes off for money. All I hope is that we listen seriously to sex workers and accept their insights as authoritative.

I intentionally left many of these stories open-ended. While I include my own thoughts and observations, I tried mainly to be as true to the events in the clubs as I can. Some readers will see exploitation and abuse. Others will see liberation and empowerment. If I have done my job well, most readers should see both. Here lies the truth: like a woman's existence in First World twenty-first-century patriarchy, sex work is complicated. In fact, I argue that the clubs are a microcosm of the experience of being female in this culture. We find immense power through our sexuality but we are also reduced to it. We can use that objectification to gain power or we can be crushed by it.

The real world is the same: women are always judged on their sexuality, though hopefully they have other characteristics that can be recognized. My regular clients were drawn initially to how I looked, but many of them became friends on the basis of intellectual and emotional bonds that, in spite of occurring within a fantasy world, were very genuine. I learned that my sexuality does not always prevent me from being seen, heard, respected, and honored for my wit and intelligence.

Ultimately, the club allowed me to come into my power. It allowed me to heal from the intense bullying I experienced in middle school, bullying often targeted not on me as a person but on me as a *girl*. While being recognized for my intelligence in college, I was recognized as sexy in the club. I grew into a whole person nurtured by both of these environments.

Our culture tells us that women are the objects of the male gaze, that our bodies are the voids upon which men project all their fancies. This is what it means to be objectified, to have one's body become a canvas upon which the male artist draws his revenge fantasies, his secret longings, his hidden desires, his insecurities, his murderous rages. Culture makes woman a mirror reflecting the man.

But women have eyes. The mirror looks back. "Stripping encapsulates and dramatizes such personal and political issues through juxtapositions of public nudity and business suits, money and desire, youth and age, idealization and stigma, rebellion and safety" and people, particularly women, are interested because "these questions and tensions emerge within [our] everyday lives and stripping makes the contradictions of theory tangible" (Frank 507). My experience as an exotic dancer allowed me to frame academic theory within personal experience. Now, when I speak before a women's studies class, I do so with more authority than if I had not been a stripper. What others theorize, I *know*.

I know that my body is scrutinized and judged in a way that male bodies are not. I also know that I can give my words the weight of my intellect and that most people will listen when I speak confidently even if I am topless and wearing 6-inch heels. I know that my white skin is a privilege because I have seen amazing, powerful, strong women of color passed over in favor of people who look like me. I know that coming from a well-educated family that expected me to become well educated and successful in my own right separates me from women who come from impoverished backgrounds. I know that relationships between males and females and gender-fluid people can be analyzed through the feminist lens of power relations, and I also know that theories of power fall short in the face of complex human connections that form between the staff, dancers, and clientele in strip clubs. I know that the strip club is merely a microcosm of patriarchal culture in all its complexity and messiness.

The strip club is not "either" and "or." It is "both" and "and." It is neither. It is the unique experiences of each individual who has ever taken their clothes off in exchange for money.

I was raised a feminist by progressive, well-educated parents. Working as a stripper for five years allowed me to learn what it really can mean to be a feminist. Being a stripper is not the only way to live the experience of feminist theory, and not every stripper has the same experience as I did. But it is part of my journey and I would not take it back for the world.

I am a trajectory, a journey. In grade school I had friends, but I proved too different for middle-school conformity. I wore weird clothes, I had been too many places, I spoke too precisely. The beauty of the Ozark mountain wilderness is corrupted by small-mindedness. By seventh grade the attacks had become vicious, tearing down everything that gave me a sense of identity: the way I dressed, the books I read, the way I looked. I began to fear school with a terror so thick I could taste it. I tried to make myself small and become invisible.

But I can't. My personality is too big. I can't stop wearing the flamboyant clothes I love, speaking my mind, showing my intelligence. By eighth grade I feared even stepping into the hallways. I can only remember those halls as dark, monsters in the shadows. I survived only by escaping.

Thirteen years old, I dance with my shadow, music player in hand, breathless, in love with the rhythm of my own body moving, music in my head. I stretch in silhouette, watching my form thin, admiring my rounding hips and upturned breasts. My shadow is the image I see in the magazines I smuggle into my room, long-legged, flawless, reflection of the youth our culture worships. My shade on the wall is perfection, not what I see when I look in the mirror. I am Narcissus, falling in love with the illusion of what I think I want to become.

Nineteen years old, I step onto stage for the first time, the unfamiliar feel of a G-string cupping my body, forbidden and erotic arousal tingling through me. In the last five years in high school and college I learned the power of my sexuality, the control I gain by teasing and withholding. This is the test of that power, pushing the limits past societal taboo. I am everything repression fears and I love it. The heavy beat builds in the powerful sound system and the music sweeps me away. I do not see the men watching, only my body reflected in the mirrors from every angle, skin glistening with sweat and oil. The man before me leans forward, sliding bills toward me but I look past him, admiring the effect of the lights in my golden hair. I am stripper Barbie, a parody of the American teenager, deranged, Kali on a death trip. I see the admiration in the eyes watching me, proving that I am as beautiful as I always wanted to be, transformed by makeup and high-heeled shoes.

On my twenty-first birthday I roll in money. Bills stick to my skin and I sit up on hands and knees as music screams through me on the cheers of the crowd. The metal heels of my 5-inch stilettos sparkle in the strobe lights, and I pound myself down on the stage, drunk with lust for myself. A man sitting at the stage throws a handful of money and the bills fall like confetti. I laugh, rocking back on my heels, bent at the waist, looking between my legs at the pulsing crowd. I am sex incarnate. I am a drug. I am the most powerful woman who has ever lived.

The stage is covered in money and more falls around me, tossed by a crowd standing five people deep around the stage. The screaming rises above the music and I somersault backward out of the splits, brushing away the money sticking to my skin. This is almost better than sex. I slip the straps of my G-string low on my waist, thrusting my hips into the air, loving the way the thin black cloth outlines my pelvis, stretching across my hipbones. I pinch my nipples to keep them hard, rubbing the glitter coating my skin, watching myself in the mirror above the stage. A hundred-dollar bill floats down to land on my stomach and the crowd screams with approval.

I leave the stage with a grocery bag bulging with money. My hands shake with adrenaline shock and I gulp deliriously at the sweet drink someone shoves in my hand. Counting the money later, I will discover that I have made more than $1200 in ten minutes; I leave the club that night with $1900 in ones and fives, twenties and hundreds. Tonight I have won. I have conquered my body image. I have molded myself into a goddess. I am Athena stripped, brilliant, powerful, untouchable. I have become my own Jungian shadow. The child frightened of going to school for fear of the older boys roaming the junior-high halls has become the ghost.

Chapter Twenty-Three

Into the Deep

The stripper is not solely the passive object of the masculine gaze. She maintains agency through her own watchful eye.
— Alexandra G. Murphy

A lot of the literature and research on sex workers denies us agency. The irony is that patriarchy denies women agency and academics participate in the denial by asserting truths about the experiences of sex workers that may not dovetail with what the workers themselves report. Of course, an outsider's perspective is valuable in any ethnographic endeavor, but the most we can say is that the truth is somewhere between what sex workers describe and what researchers see.

Researchers who study sex work are most often female graduate students (Frank 2007). They approach their work from one of two standpoints: radical feminist or sex-positive feminism, sometimes called progressive feminism (Williams 1989; Barton 2000). Radical feminists argue that women are not only objectified in patriarchal culture but often participate in their own subjugation. Radical feminists thus conclude that strippers are abused, from dysfunctional backgrounds, and lie to themselves about their position in society, leading to self-medication and psychological trauma.

Sex-positive feminists see stripping as a way for women to take control of their bodies, recognize and deconstruct prescribed gender roles, and seek liberation from patriarchal norms that desexualize women. What both sides have in common is that "feminist theory itself deploys an analysis of power, gendered and otherwise, as a central problematic" (Frank 507). Power is most often understood as an either/or dialectic: if one person gains power then another loses it. The two feminist standpoints "suggest an either/or problematic, in which stripping is either heteronormative or liberating" (Pilcher 523). The possibility that it is *both* is less often recognized. Furthermore, the possibility that a woman can be empowered in such a way that no one loses power, or gives her power, but that she finds and nurtures it within herself is completely overlooked. "One might expect feminists and sociologists to be more nuanced and less caricaturing of their attitudes toward strippers...feminist research and theories on sex work have been monopolized by two equally extreme and reductionist positions" (Barton 585–6), and it is time we gain a more nuanced and complex understanding of the reality of the subset of modern culture where women sell their sexuality.

I was a feminist before I became a stripper. I was also young and didn't fully understand what feminism meant. Privileged by my white skin and educated family background, I had never recognized sexism as a factor in my own life. Patriarchy was something that affected other people. By engaging objectification on my own terms with intentionality (because my privilege allows me to do so), I came to a much more nuanced understanding of what it means to be female, and white, in this culture. Katy Pilcher (2012) discovered that "dancers expect to be objects of a sexualized 'gaze' at work, but outside of this space they seek to challenge ideas about women's bodies as sexual objects" (532). By profiting from being treated as a sexual object I learned to challenge sexualization.

I also learned that being seen as sexy is fun. It is fun to play, and flirt, and tease. Girls are taught by our culture that our value lies in being seen as desirable by males. I learned how to take control of how men see me, how to communicate with men who view me as alluring, and how to negotiate in order to get my needs met. The men who became my regular customers came to see me as more than a pretty face.

The lessons I learned inside the clubs have served me well

both professionally and in my relationships. As long as all parties engage consensually in sexualized play, even as a financial transaction, it can teach us about our own desires, boundaries, and preferred ways of being in the world. The presence of money in this business is typically seen as a coercive factor that either disempowers the women who perform for it or the customer who is manipulated out of it. In my experience the financial exchange was understood by both parties, and, like any other transaction, it is an exchange that benefits both people. The vast majority of clients with whom I interacted understood exactly what they were buying and the game in which they were engaged with me. We all participated willingly in the construction of a fantasy. And we recognized the fantasy for what it was. Only rarely did someone mistake reality in the club for reality in the outside world.

The male gaze is considered to objectify women and serve as a form of control in that the woman performs for him. However, this entirely overlooks the fact that strippers are not objects: we look back. Furthermore, stripping often plays with "traditional" female roles such as the housewife, the librarian, and the schoolgirl. But the reason these roles are sexy is because they are considered asexual and, as the clothing is removed, the sexuality is revealed. The transformation of the asexual Victorian stereotype into the sexual adult female is transgressive in that female sexuality is celebrated. And this matters even when the male client doesn't realize it. Because what he's experiencing is separate from the dancer's experience. Her experience is completely her own. To define her experience through the lens of the male customer perpetuates the misogynist stereotypes that feminism is supposed to identify and deconstruct. Finally, though studies on frequenters of strip clubs are sparse, "customers themselves are quite critical of their own engagement with the dancing" (Pilcher 533). Customers are not (typically) slavering, animalistic men. Some of them are women. Most of them are self-reflective and engaged. "Men frequent strip clubs not only to watch women dance, but also for male homosociality, as men may experience a sense of 'communal ecstasy' from collectively watching a taboo activity," Pilcher notes (531). I'd add that it's not just a "taboo activity"; people seek a sense of camaraderie in sporting events, concerts, conventions, and conferences. Customers get to know one another; they form friendships with one another and the staff of clubs. We support one another; we've got each other's backs.

So many researchers approach strip clubs, and sex work, as if the conditions are somehow unique. There are very few research projects on stripping that actively compare this work with other occupations that overtly objectify women: modeling, hostessing in restaurants, cocktail waitressing, ballet, and acting being likely candidates for comparison. The research that does attempt comparison does so within the realm of sex work, drawing conclusions about the differences between different realms of sex work. While this is valuable, it overlooks that women are always objectified, no matter what we're doing or how much clothing we're wearing. Strip clubs are not much different from the rest of society; in fact, they're a microcosm in which patriarchal culture can be clearly understood.

The greatest benefit I received from working as a stripper is that I learned firsthand how gender norms are constructed. I learned that "stripping is at least potentially transgressive through exposing the instability of gender and showing that it is performative rather than 'natural'" (Pilcher 523). I am grateful for the insights I gained that have allowed me to be very intentional about how I understand myself and represent myself to others. As a heterosexual female I had never considered other options prior to entering the permissive environs of the strip club. I gained a deep appreciation for the diversity of female beauty and human sexual expression. I found that the clubs in which I worked also allowed space for customers to express their sexuality in a variety of ways. I became more open-minded and accepting. As Pilcher writes, "erotic dance is situated within, yet potentially disruptive of, traditional heteronormative and hetero-patriarchal boundaries" (522).

Another valuable lesson is that I gained a much more nuanced understanding of power. I alluded to some of these realizations previously, and I'll add that I became aware that sexual power can be liberating or degrading depending on context. Some people look at a woman's marketing of her sexuality as inherently demeaning. Barton (2002) notes that dancers understand themselves "as the power figures at the same time that [they] explained [their] strategies for dealing with men who do not respect [them]. Such a seeming contradiction is, indeed, the reality of daily experience for most strippers" (594). These experiences taught me to negotiate the realities of being a *woman* in a profession. I have been dismissed by colleagues and even students for being female, and I have a much better grasp of strategies to address being discounted merely because of my sex. I often joke with my friends that stripping was a great crash course in politics that set me up to be successful in the highly political environment of academics. Ex-stripper Erika Lyremark wrote a book titled *Think Like a Stripper: Business Lessons to Up Your Confidence, Attract More Clients & Rule Your Market* (2013) in which she applies the lessons she learned dancing to business strategy and negotiation. Patriarchy disempowers women. Stripping taught me how to take my power back.

Reading Questions

1. What do you think this book is about? What does the author claim it's about?
2. The author never defines feminism. What do you think feminism means to her? How do you think she defines it?
3. The author writes about her own privileges—education, economic class, race. Do you think her privilege affects how she understands and defines feminism? If so, how?
4. One of the researchers cited by the author says that dancers must "acknowledge and rewrite their subjugated sexual narratives in more positive and empowered ways" (Philaretou 48). The author goes on to refute this claim, instead arguing that real power can be found by strippers. But is she simply "rewriting" her "subjugated sexual narrative"?
5. The author claims that strip clubs are "a microcosm in which patriarchal culture can be clearly understood." What does she mean? Are there lessons about modern culture that can be learned from this book?
6. In what specific ways did the author grow as a person as a result of working in strip clubs? As an academic?

Bibliography

Barton, Bernadette. "Dancing on the Möbius Strip: Challenging the Sex War Paradigm." *Gender & Society*, Vol. 16, no. 5 (2002): 585–602.

Bernard, Constance, Christen DeGabrielle, Lynette Cartier, Elizabeth Monk-Turner, Celestine Phil, Jennifer Sherwood, and Thomasena Tyree. "Exotic Dancers: Gender Differences in Social Reaction, Subcultural Ties, and Conventional Support." *Journal of Criminal Justice and Popular Culture*, Vol. 10, no. 1 (2003): 1–11.

Brooks, Peter. *Body Work: Objects of Desire in Modern Narrative*. Cambridge: Harvard University Press, 1993.

Downs, Daniel M., Shaan James, and Gloria Cowan. "Body Objectification, Self-Esteem, and Relationship Satisfaction: A Comparison of Exotic Dancers and College Women." *Sex Roles*, Vol. 54, no. 11 (2006): 745–52.

Frank, Katherine. "Thinking Critically about Strip Club Research." *Sexualities*, Vol. 10, no. 4 (2007): 501–17.

Lilleston, Pamela, Jacqueline Reuben, and Susan G. Sherman. "'This Is Our Sanctuary': Perceptions of Safety among Exotic Dancers in Baltimore, Maryland." *Health Place* (2012): 1–14.

Lyremark, Erika. *Think Like a Stripper: Business Lessons to Up Your Confidence, Attract More Clients & Rule Your Market*. Minneapolis: Bascom Hill Publishing Group, 2013.

Maticka-Tyndale, Eleanor, Jacqueline Lewis, Jocalyn P. Clark, Jennifer Zubick, and Shelley Young. "Women and Health." *Women and Health*, Vol. 31 (2000): 87–108.

Moore, Eva, Jennifer Han, Christine Serio-Chapman, Cynthia Mobley, Catherine Watson, and Mishka Terplan. "Contraception and Clean Needles: Feasibility of Combining Mobile Reproductive Health and Needle Exchange for Female Exotic Dancers." *The American Journal of Public Health*, Vol.

102, no. 10 (2012): 1833–6.

Mulvey, Laura. *Visual and Other Pleasures*. London: Macmillan Press, 1989.

Murphy, Alexandra G. "The Dialectical Gaze: Exploring the Subject-Object Tension in the Performances of Women Who Strip." *Journal of Contemporary Ethnography*, Vol. 32, no. 3 (2003): 305–35.

Philaretou, Andreas G. "Female Exotic Dancers: Intrapersonal and Interpersonal Perspectives." *Sexual Addiction and Compulsivity*, Vol. 13, no. 1 (2006): http://dx.doi.org/10.10 80/10720160500529243

Pilcher, Katy. "Dancing for Women: Subverting Heteronormativity in a Lesbian Erotic Dance Space?" *Sexualities* (2012): 521–37.

Weitzer, Ronald, ed. *Sex for Sale: Prostitution, Pornography, and the Sex Industry*. New York: Routledge, 2000.

Wesely, Jennifer K. "Exotic Dancing and Negotiation of Identity: The Multiple Uses of Body Technologies." *Journal of Contemporary Ethnography*, Vol. 32, no. 6 (2003): 643–69.

Williams, Linda. *Hardcore: Power, Pleasure, and the "Frenzy of the Visible."* Berkeley: University of California Press, 1989.

CHANGE
MAKERS
BOOKS

Changemakers Books

TRANSFORMATION

Transform your life, transform your world – Changemakers Books publishes for individuals committed to transforming their lives and transforming the world. Our readers seek to become positive, powerful agents of change. Changemakers Books inform, inspire, and provide practical wisdom and skills to empower us to write the next chapter of humanity's future.

If you have enjoyed this book, why not tell other readers by posting a review on your preferred book site. Recent bestsellers from Changemakers Books are:

Integration
The Power of Being Co-Active in Work and Life
Ann Betz, Karen Kimsey-House
Integration examines how we came to be polarized in our dealing with self and other, and what we can do to move from an either/or state to a more effective and fulfilling way of being.
Paperback: 978-1-78279-865-1 ebook: 978-1-78279-866-8

Bleating Hearts
The Hidden World of Animal Suffering
Mark Hawthorne
An investigation of how animals are exploited for entertainment, apparel, research, military weapons, sport, art, religion, food, and more.
Paperback: 978-1-78099-851-0 ebook: 978-1-78099-850-3

Lead Yourself First!
Indispensable Lessons in Business and in Life
Michelle Ray
Are you ready to become the leader of your own life? Apply simple, powerful strategies to take charge of yourself, your career, your destiny.
Paperback: 978-1-78279-703-6 ebook: 978-1-78279-702-9

Burnout to Brilliance
Strategies for Sustainable Success
Jayne Morris
Routinely running on reserves? This book helps you transform your life from burnout to brilliance with strategies for sustainable success.
Paperback: 978-1-78279-439-4 ebook: 978-1-78279-438-7

The Master Communicator's Handbook
Teresa Erickson, Tim Ward
Discover how to have the most communicative impact in this guide by professional communicators with over 30 years of experience advising leaders of global organizations.
Paperback: 978-1-78535-153-2 ebook: 978-1-78535-154-9

Meditation in the Wild
Buddhism's Origin in the Heart of Nature
Charles S. Fisher Ph.D.
A history of Raw Nature as the Buddha's first teacher, inspiring some followers to retreat there in search of truth.
Paperback: 978-1-78099-692-9 ebook: 978-1-78099-691-2

Ripening Time
Inside Stories for Aging with Grace
Sherry Ruth Anderson
Ripening Time gives us an indispensable guidebook for growing
into the deep places of wisdom as we age.
Paperback: 978-1-78099-963-0 ebook: 978-1-78099-962-3

Striking at the Roots
A Practical Guide to Animal Activism
Mark Hawthorne
A manual for successful animal activism from an author with first-
hand experience speaking out on behalf of animals.
Paperback: 978-1-84694-091-0 ebook: 978-1-84694-653-0

Voices of the Sacred Feminine
Conversations to Re-Shape Our World
Rev. Dr. Karen Tate
If we can envision it, we can manifest it! Discover conversations
that help us begin to re-shape the world!
Paperback: 978-1-78279-510-0 ebook: 978-1-78279-509-4

Readers of ebooks can buy or view any of these bestsellers by
clicking on the live link in the title. Most titles are published in
paperback and as an ebook. Paperbacks are available in traditional
bookshops. Both print and ebook formats are available online.

Find more titles and sign up to our readers' newsletter at
http://www.johnhuntpublishing.com/transformation
Follow us on Facebook at
https://www.facebook.com/Changemakersbooks